Life is Uncharted Territory

Stories of a Vietnam Army Nurse

by
Judy Crausbay Hamilton

Life is Uncharted Territory

Copyright © 2019 by Judy Crausbay Hamilton

All rights reserved. Except as permitted under the U.S. Copyright Act of 1976, no part of this publication may be produced, distributed, or transmitted in any form or by any means, or stored in a database or retrieval system, without the prior written permission of the publisher.

ISBN: 978-1-6865-8752-8

Printed in the United States of America

*"Do not go where the path may lead,
go instead where there is no path and leave a trail."*

—Ralph Waldo Emerson

Contents

1: These Boots Were Made for Walking 1
2: Sisters 3
3: The Flight When I Kissed Death 7
4: The ANG Squadron 11
5: Rapid Decompression 13
6: It Is What It Is 21
7: Army Nurse Corps 25
8: The Field Grade Officer 29
9: Monterey…California 33
10: Bing Cherries 37
11: Ft. Ord and Bill Greiner 41
12: Home Sweet Home 45
13: Horny 49
14: Fragging 53
15: Susie 57
16 : The Ward 59
17: Merry Christmas, Mom and Dad 63
18: Welcome to MARS 65
19: A Mystery 69
20: Whistle Dixie 75
21: Just Three Pounds 81
22: Flak Jacket 83
23: Then There is Red 89
24: "Rock" 91
25: TACOS 95
26: SAPPER Attack 99

27: Wingman 103
28: R and R 107
29: HERCULES 111
30: A Marine Firebase Camp 115
31: When a Lady Has To Pee 117
32: Montagnard Smiles 119
33: The Green Beret Medic 125
34: Green Beret Sleep Over 127
35: The Aussie and the Bomb 129
36: The Day is Still Young 133
37: The Ravens 137
38: Letter from a Patient 141
39: Leaving Vietnam 143
40: Hello 'Grunt' 145
41: Epilogue 149

1

These Boots Were Made for Walking

The song sung by Nancy Sinatra was a hit, played on the Armed Forces Radio. Nancy donned bright, white, knee-high boots while entertaining troops serving in Vietnam. We girl soldiers could long for such fancy duds as they were certainly more feminine than boots issued to women in the Army Nurse Corps. I was issued a size seven, the smallest size in the Quartermasters' gear. To compensate for the over-sized boots, I slid my foot into the boot wearing two standard Army green socks on each foot.

My black boots are worn and have lost their luster. Not to be outdone by Nancy, as I wore my fatigues and my issued black boots during long hours of caring for our wounded soldiers. Truth. My boots were part of my uniform as I walked all over Vietnam. They hitch hiked from Saigon to where I worked at the 29th Evac Hospital in the Mekong Delta. My boots explored a tribal

Montagnard village and ended up spending a long memorable night in the Central Highlands of Vietnam guarded by America's finest, the Green Berets.

I spent the day with Tuy Hoa C-130 Squadron as they flew a medical crew to transport wounded GI's from MASH units in I Corps, near the DMZ, to the 95th Evac Hospital at DaNang.

And my boots made many trips to Tuy Hoa Air Base where I spent off duty time with friends in the 309th and the 188th. I wore my fatigues and combat boots as a girl amongst men, trying to be incognito while enjoying the company of 'flyguys.'

And as the war took its toll, my war weary boots made several long walks to Tuy Hoa to wish my friends a last good-bye. In the weariness of caring for combat wounded, American soldiers and wounded Vietnamese, my boots knelt in prayer and prayed for… peace.

2

Sisters

The journey of my life began when as a young girl, our mother died. I am in the first grade and my sister is in the second grade when our dad enrolled, his girls in a Catholic boarding school. This is my first encounter with a Catholic Nun. They are mysterious women. Their hands and faces are pink alright, but I am curious to know if the rest of their body is pink. I'm not even sure they have bodies as their black robes hang all the way to the floor.

One night I asked my sister, "Donna, do you think the nuns have legs under their robes?"

"Of course, they do, Judy, how do you think they walk?"

"I just wonder that's all."

In a sleepy voice she replied, "Judy, go to sleep. I'm tired."

That night I morph into a six-year-old sleuth; I want to know for myself if the nuns have arms and legs. I'm scared, but not scared enough. As I scoot across the floor to lie on my back on the cold linoleum floor. I take in a deep breath and pull up the bottom of the nuns curtain.

"What if she sees me looking at her?" Anxiety did not rule, as a bravado beyond my years egg me on. I said to myself, "I just know the Nun's legs and arms are as black as her robe!" I am disappointed to see that the skin on her arms is pink! The same pink as my arms! The bravado that pushed me into this adventure dissipated and the floor is cold and scary. I scurry back to my bed. I didn't get to see the nun's legs still; I am certain, beyond a doubt, the Nun's legs are as black as her robe.

Donna and I had been a Catholic and a Methodist. I studied in four schools from the first through the sixth grade. When I am eleven, Daddy married Pearl, a woman as beautiful as her name. Our blended family left New Orleans and moved to Irving, Texas where Mama gave birth to our baby sister, Sharon, a sweet baby. She was well loved by the whole family.

Best of all, my Grandma Gregg (mother's mother) lived close to us, in Waxahachie. Our Grandma told us that Jesus is kind and he knows all about our lives. If Jesus knows about our lives, then we want to know about him. Donna and I knelt at Grandma's knees and asked Jesus to come into our hearts.

Then on a spring day, just shy of my twentieth birthday, it happened:

A lie! A hoax! Funny…not! Judy, your sister Donna was in an auto accident and she did not survive! There, I heard it again…that capricious trick!

My heart was shattered! Beyond repair shattered! A janitor, a student at the college I attend, opened the empty chapel of worship. Where I walked to the altar and collapsed into a puddle of tears.

"God! My sister…dead! I can't go on without her! Are you listening God? We survived our mother's death, the Catholic nuns, and living in so many places. As young girls in west Texas, we looked at puffy white clouds in a blue sky and pretended Mother sat on a soft cloud, watching and loving on her girls."

My soul fell to the depth of sorrow as I lift my head and cried.

"In college; we worked the swing-shift, as nurse-aides, getting to bed at midnight, only to be up for early morning classes. God! We were strong together. Donna and I held hands as we walked the circuitous path of our lives.

My sister…dead…there was no one to hold my hand. No one knows me, and no one really cares about me, not-even-God!

My tears drove my stomach into an ulcer. I downed milk to appease the hole in my stomach and continued my studies to be a nurse. With a lump in my throat and a knot in my gut I grieved of life without my sister. I didn't even know when the searing pain in my heart lessen, as for years, the skies of my life were void of puffy white clouds, as a swirling storm tore at my soul. I woke each morning with an ache in my heart that dulled, ever so slow. The memories of my childhood and the memories of my sister lay dormant somewhere deep in my heart.

3

The Flight When I Kissed Death

I have no memory of feeling alone when my mother died. My sister Donna cried for both of us. Jesus lost his place in my heart. As crazy as it may seem, if God had been there, then my sister would be alive. It's been two years since Donna died. *There must be more to life than crying inside over my sister's death.*

While at work, I made myself smile. A co-worker blew my cover when she told me, "Judy, I know what could pull you out of depression. I joined the Air National Guard and I like it. Check it out; maybe it's a fit for you."

"You're in the Air Force, and you work here, at the Children's Hospital?" I asked.

"It's not full-time military duty," she said. "Here's how it goes: I give the Guard one weekend a month and two weeks every year. And, best of all, I get to fly all over in large airplanes."

A nurse in the Guard? Qualifying as an Air Force flight nurse intrigued me, so, without much thought, my roomie Carol and I joined the Air National Guard. We were the newest Flight nurses. I have always lived life near the edge, so being part of the Air National Guard suits me well.

My first long-distance flight happened like this. My name, along with Anne's, is on the flight manifest: destination Elmendorf AB in Fairbanks, Alaska. The mission: to transport a platoon of the Montana Army Guard, part of the storied 163rd Armored Cavalry, from their two-week training in Alaska back to their home in Montana. This is my first lengthy flight with our squadron, the Oklahoma Air National Guard.

Color me proud.

When we land at Fairbanks, Alaska, the loadmaster says, "You should try to rest, as we may load the troops and do a quick turnaround."

"The pilots? When do they rest?" I ask.

"They fly with an extra crew to spot them, so the ones flying are not the same pilots that bring our plane home," he explains.

Try to rest? I am tired; still, adventure pulsates through my veins. I am at the top of the earth, in Alaska, where in July the sun never sets. My billet is a room with the windows draped in heavy, dull, black curtains. I tell myself; *I will just relax a few minutes. I am way too excited to sleep.*

What do I know? As a knock on the door startles me awake. The voice at the door said, "Lieutenant meet us at the flight line. We are ready to go."

Would they leave without me? I don't want to know. I hustle to meet the flight crew, with no time to spare.

Our passengers are bone tired and ready to go home. The men strap in tight along both sides of the ribbed metal interior of the C-130. One soldier, with a broken leg, is on a litter in the metal stanchion in the center of the fuselage. I am standing beside his litter and think: *this flight is bumpy, sort of like a car driving over a dry, washboard dirt road.*

As I am on my first long flight with the Air Guard, I thought that rough air was standard, when the tail of the plane went nearly vertical. I white-knuckled my grip on the stretcher, when up went the tail again. I lost my grip on the stretcher and flew like a limp ragdoll toward the back of the plane when a National Guardsman, as smooth as an outfielder catching a baseball, reached out and caught me! He wrapped his burly arms around me and held on tight. He saved my life!

When the Oklahoma military air taxi arrived in Billings, Montana, all the soldiers stood up. I didn't know who to thank for saving my life as they all wore crumpled Army fatigues.

With "mission accomplished," our pilots flew their filly back to Oklahoma City. The flight through the thunderstorms was enough for Anne, the nurse with me, as the mission to Alaska was her last flight. She left military nursing and never looked back.

The scary flight through the thunderstorms changed me, as I was up to the challenge. I stayed the course and earned my Flight Nurse wings. Best of all, grieving over Donna's death lessened, when I slowly stepped away from the shadow of depression and turned to look up.

4

The ANG Squadron

The people in the Air Guard are family to me. The memory of Clay and his two sick cows' reigns. It happened on Saturday of 'Guard' week-end; four-o-clock rolls around, and we all enjoyed a beer or two at the pub. When Clay blurted out,

"It's dark and I've sick cows to tend to!"

"Sick Cows Clay? I'm a nurse, I can help." I said.

A carload of not-quite-sober-Guardsmen drove to Clay's place in the country *to 'help' him tend to his sick cows*. We walked in the front door, said hello to his stunned wife, and walked straight out the back door, to tend to the cows. Clay could ill afford to give costly penicillin injections to all the cows so, to locate the two that were sick, we had to find the two cows that had a fever.

Now, to take the temperature of a cow (recall it is dark) requires four Guardsmen; one to hold the flashlight, one to lift the cow's tail and one to insert a very long thermometer into the cow's backside. I was not as 'soused' as the rest of the Guardsmen and could tell where *'taking-the-cows-temp'* was going. So, I declared, "I'm a Texan, and I'm an experienced 'cow-whisperer'" as I moved toward the cow's head.

There are tamer memories that happened with the Air Guard squadron; watching a dance show in Puerto Rico starring Marlena Dietrich, and in Greece walking the hills that Apostle Paul walked. None of my Guard memories are as bizarre as the evening we Air Guardsmen spent with Clay Hembree and his sick cows. Really happened, yes, it did.

Of course, I spent time flying in the Air Guard C-130 learning and practicing to better myself as an Air Force Flight nurse. I didn't have my sites on Army nursing, but what do I know?

The Air National Guard is my first intro to military nursing. And it came about as a result of my sister's death as before she died, I was a happy-go-lucky gal, just working and dating and enjoying both. An example of when a tragic happening in my life pushed me to look up. Like Neil Diamond sings, thank the Lord for the nighttime, I thank the Lord for you.

5

Rapid Decompression

I shudder when I think of the flight Anne and I made coming back to Oklahoma from Alaska. The orders I received today read: "Lieutenant Judy Crausbay will work with the 388th Aeromed Squadron in Yokota, Japan."

I locate Staff Sergeant Howenstein, whose name is also on my orders, to ask, "But, Sergeant, does the Air Force realize that I am a brand-new flight nurse? I just didn't expect this so soon."

Sergeant Howenstein tried to dispel my fear. "It will be okay, Lieutenant," he assures me. "You will work alongside experienced flight nurses, and I will do the same with Air Force non-com medical crew. Why, we may not even see each other until our flight back to Oklahoma."

Our two-week active Guard duty began at Travis Airforce Base, California, when we board a C-141, a large jet-propelled Air Force Military Air Transport plane, destination Yokota, Japan.

The C-141 Starlifter had a dual mission: to bring supplies to Vietnam and to carry combat wounded from Vietnam. I learned a military term: dead-head: except for the flight crew, and we three Air Guard people, the fuselage of the massive jet plane was empty.

When the plane leveled off at an altitude of 35,000 feet, I was invited by the Aircraft Commander (the AC) to join the crew on the flight-deck.

I was pumped. I strapped myself in the jump seat between the AC and the co-pilot. The Milky Way seemed close enough to reach out and run my hand through it. Inside myself, I sang the line of a hymn, Oh, Lord my God, when I in awesome wonder, consider all the worlds thy hands have made.

Our MATS aircraft C-141 landed at Wake Island, a strategic Pacific island that made history in the Pacific during World War II. We deplaned to stretch our legs while our plane was refueled. The flight crew and we three Air Guardsmen walked past another C-141 parked on the tarmac. The massive rear doors of this Starlifter were gone. The doors were just not there! We stare at the ragged edges, where the cargo doors had been torn off. An eerie quiet consumed us as though we were at a wake. The thick padding along the sides of the plane and the padded seats had been ripped out. I was mesmerized by globs of pink insulation floating, like graceful ballerinas, about the empty hull. We were speechless as we walked away from the lifeless plane to Base Ops.

Our Aircraft Commander leaned into the half window, to not miss a word of the clerk's excited response. "Yes, sir, they landed forty minutes ago. I understand the plane reached thirty-five thousand feet, when the cargo doors just flat blew off."

The airman went on to say, "It's only by the grace of God that out of the flight crew and eighty passengers, only one man was injured. Only one man out of eighty! Can you believe it?"

"We are dead-heading," our pilot replied. "We have a medical crew with us. If need be, we can take the GIs on to Vietnam. I need to talk with the AC of the damaged plane."

A medical crew, he was referring to we three Air Guardsmen. I wondered if I should tell him that the NCO' (non-commissioned officers) on our team had logged more years and flight time than I have? The gold bars on my uniform designate me as the team leader. I took a deep breath and felt my stomach churning.

Our Aircraft Commander turned to me to detail the mission. "Lieutenant, you evaluate the injured man and get back to me ASAP. I will meet with the commander of the damaged aircraft and wait for you here in Ops."

An Air Force jeep whisked me away from the wounded C-141 to the base infirmary, a small clinic with an exam room. On entering the clinic, I saw a man thrashing about on a gurney, like a child with a fever.

"How long has he been doing this?" I asked the man in the room. I assumed I was talking to a doctor. "Since he got here," the doctor replied.

"Have you given him any meds?"

"I don't have medication that will help Justin."

"Justin? His name is Justin?" I asked the doctor.

"Justin is the name on his DL."

I leaned toward Justin's ear. "Justin! Justin! Can you hear me? Squeeze my hand, Justin. Can . . . you . . . squeeze . . . my . . . hand?"

He does not respond. I turn to the doctor to ask, "Do you have a ball-point pen?"

He hands me the pen from his shirt pocket,

I mark the point of the pen down the length of the inside of Justin's foot. A person with full neurologic sensation would curl his toes. Justin's toes go wide open, like an old hand-held church fan.

I talk to Justin as though he understands me. "I am going to measure your BP, Justin." Then somewhere in the coils of my brain ran the core of a lecture: "When scuba diving below thirty feet, bubbles in the blood system are compressed. On a rapid ascension, a bubble expands, and the diver has the 'bends.' This law inverts when an aircraft loses cabin pressure. A bubble expands and can lodge in the brain."

I turn to the doctor to ask, "Is there an ambulance on the island to bring Justin to our airplane? As he needs a decompression chamber."

The airman that brought me to the clinic was waiting to take me back to OPS, where I met with the Commander of our C-141.

"Sir, I do not have good news. The injured man may have a cerebral embolus, an air bubble, blocking the blood flow in his head. His survival depends on how quickly he gets to a decompression chamber."

"A decompression chamber. That serious, Lieutenant?"

"Yes, sir."

"Okay, then." His response was measured. "The closest decompression chamber is at the Naval Medical Center in Hawaii. I will instruct our loadmaster to get the passengers boarded and we will be airborne."

We loaded the GIs onto our C-141 and the massive rear doors closed tight. I read raw fear in their faces, hoping this C-141 will not explode like the plane they were on.

Our team of two Air Guardsmen had Justin secured on a litter close to the rear cargo doors, when the color drained from the face of my sergeant.

He hollered over the roar of engines to say, "The normal cabin pressure at altitude is five to seven thousand feet."

I turned my head, searching for lost cabin pressure when the sergeant's remark registered. Oh, God! Justin's grip on life was fragile and he would die when blood clot expands to match the cabin pressure.

My sergeant had detected a life-altering situation before it happened. For sure he had logged more flying hours than I, and I was very glad he was part of our Air Guard team.

"Gotta talk to the Aircraft Commander!" I raced the length of the fuselage to the flight deck and saw that our Aircraft Commander and his co-pilot were in the middle of the strategic preflight check. I had flown on several flights with the Air Guard and knew full well that there was an unwritten rule that no one interrupts the pilot's and co-pilot's focus when they were in the middle of the preflight check list.

I broke the rule. I tapped ever so lightly on the shoulder of the Aircraft Commander. "Sir?"

"What!" He turned his head and responded in a terse tone.

"The cabin pressure at altitude."

"What about it, Lieutenant?"

"The cabin pressure needs to be low." I knew what I wanted to tell him, yet my mouth was dry, and my words tumbled over each other. "Elevated altitude lets the bubble in Justin's head expand."

Our pilot caught on quickly and said to the co-pilot, "Our cabin pressure is six thousand feet. Let's override it. This baby can fly with a cabin pressure at a negative thousand feet. We will all have headaches. Peanuts!"

"Thank you, sir. I apologize for interrupting you."

"It's okay, Lieutenant. Do you have any more bombs to drop?"

He made a joke! Our AC diffused a crisis with quick wit. I smiled as I knew we were in good hands.

Flying time to Hawaii was five hours. The flight seemed longer than usual when our medical team resorted to basic nursing skills just to keep Justin alive. At one point, his heartbeat spun out of control; I had no shock equipment, nor cardiac meds, to convert this racing rhythm. I tried a last-ditch effort and pressed simultaneously on his eyeballs. I prayed the carotid arteries behind the eyes would reset his heart rate. It worked! I am most surprised. I breathed a sigh of relief when Justin's heart regulated to a measurable tachycardiac rhythm. I made another run to the flight deck to consult, per radio, with a Navy physician in Hawaii. He assured me that, "the Navy has a decompression chamber waiting for Justin." Our C-141 received priority landing and the Navy met our plane on the flight line. With relief, I transferred Jason's care to the skillful hands of U.S.Navy doctors. When I looked toward the 79 GIs, I placed myself in their shoes.

The GI passengers boarded in California and flew to Wake Island. Then the disaster occurred, a rapid decompression at 35,000 feet over Wake Island. At Wake Island, the GIs boarded another aircraft (the same type as the C-141 that lost pressure), and they flew to Hawaii. They still had a lengthy flight to Vietnam, where one or all may die in combat.

We three Air Guardsmen had been busy, and we still hadn't made it to Japan. No downtime for us as we were on the next flight out of Hickam AB. Destination Yokota, Japan. I breathed a prayer that we would survive the thirteen days left on our TDY orders. (Training Duty)

News travels fast, especially bad news. The emergency flight from Wake Island to Hawaii was the talk of the Aeromed Squadron in Japan. Understandably, as the C-141 is "the" medical transport in the Pacific Command.

The flight nurses and senior NCOs asked me to detail the flight transporting the injured man from Wake Island to Hawaii. Detailed is a kind verb. I was grilled.

"Why did you not give the patient IV valium?"

"There was no valium."

"No valium! Then what did you use to control the seizures?"

I countered with, "The doctor had no meds to give me."

"Well, you should have insisted! And refused to take the patient without Valium!"

I was tired and totally unprepared to deal with confrontation. I realized the Aeromedical Squadron facing me were experts in their field, and I blundered into their area of expertise.

Twelve days! We had twelve days left on our orders until we could return home to the caring folks of 137th Oklahoma Air Guard. Two weeks a year. When Carol and I signed on with the Air Guard, two weeks a year seemed like a walk in the park.

An applaud happened, from an Air Force flight nurse at Goose

AB, Labrador. Her letter offset the negative reception we received from the Squadron in Japan.

DEPARTMENT OF THE AIR FORCE
868th Medical Group (SAC)
APO NEW YORK 09677
Letter of Congratulations

5 June 1966
DEPARTMENT OF THE AIR FORCE
868th Medical Group (SAC)
APO NEW YORK 09677

Lieutenant Crausbay,

I am presently assigned at Goose AB, Labrador, and hence quite removed from Aeromedical Evacuation, but my deep feelings will always be with the crews in the sky.

It was with pride and pleasure that I read of your "experience" on the flight in the Pacific area.

I know the commendable action of you and your team are almost routine in today's busy days of Aeromedical Evacuation, yet that one great asset, common sense, which you displayed so admirably, is a rare gift and one in which you should be proud.

Hearing and reading of situations such as yours makes me grateful that I was privileged to have a small part in the training of so many flight nurses.

Your actions reflect great credit not only on yourself but to your profession and to the Air National Guard. My most sincere congratulations in both your civilian and your military career.

Sincerely,
Jane M. Vino, Major, USAF NC Chief, Nursing Service

6

It Is What It Is

Excitement reigns: when Sgt. Grant and I serve our two-week active duty with the Air Force Aeromedical Squadron in beautiful Yokota, Japan, where the cherry-blossoms are in full bloom. We work alongside the Nurses and Corpsmen in the 388th Aeromed Squadron in Yokota, Japan.

I am part of the Flight Nurse team. Humble? Not. Touch me. I am a flight nurse.

The belly of the large jet aircraft is filled with supplies for Vietnam. The supplies are offloaded and in quick time the fuselage of the C-141 is loaded with combat-wounded patients. This is where I enter, as Sgt. Grant and I are part of the team that transports America's wounded from Saigon to Japan. Then we deadhead back to Ton Son Nhut (Saigon) to transport a fresh load of wounded GIs. I am dog-tired and grateful that this is our last flight.

In Yokota, Japan, the C-141 is refueled, patients are off-loaded, and a fresh group of Vietnam combat wounded are on loaded for the long flight back to the States. Sgt. Grant and I are on the manifest for our final aeromedical duty on this long over-water flight.

One of the patents occupies a canvas sling seat along the fuselage. His injury qualifies him to be a "litter-patient"; however, he has a tracheotomy (an instrument in his wind-pipe, allowing him to breathe) and were he to lie flat, mucus from his lungs would build up and he would drown.

I talk to him in my big-sister voice to say, "Someone will stay by your side to be sure you are breathing okay." With this promise, the soldier relaxes and drifts into a restless sleep. I, along with other nurses and corpsmen, kept a constant vigil over the young soldier.

He is a boy; just eighteen years old. In Basic, they taught him to fire an M-16. *But they failed to teach him how to breathe through a hole in his neck.*

The flight over the Pacific, from Japan to the air base at Anchorage, Alaska, is long. When all is quiet, we are encouraged to sit and take a load off our feet. Adrenalin pumps through my body and I cannot be still. I walk around the litter patients, play gin rummy with one patient, then walk past another man positioned in the middle of his litter. I talk to him saying, "Hello, care if I visit with you? Would you like to be pulled up on your litter? You seem uncomfortable."

The words spill out of my mouth when a split-second moment goes on forever.

The man stared long and hard, then took a deep breath to say, "I am okay where I am Ma'am, as I lost both my legs in Nam."

I turn my head to push back the bile in my throat.

"Soldier, I apologize. How rude of me."

Then the patient attempts to comfort me, when he said,

"It's okay, Ma'am, "it is what it is."

We land in Alaska, where I put on my game face. I made a decision, to serve with the Air Force in Vietnam. Am I ready to leave the nest? I am like a daughter or a sister to the guys in our squadron. Destiny calls . . . and she says, "be ready, Judy, as I will take you on the ride of your life."

7

Army Nurse Corps

I received a letter from the United States Air Force Nurse Corps in Washington, DC. It was a short message about a weighty subject:

Regarding your query about serving in Vietnam, currently the Air Force is placing nurses with rank of Captain or above in Vietnam. Your request is honorable; however, you would do well to continue to serve our country in the Air National Guard.

"Quit your bitchin', Judy," quipped a guy in my Air Guard squadron. "If the Air Force won't cut orders for Vietnam, try the Army. They'll oblige you." The Army? What a novel idea. I went by an Army Recruitment Office to learn that the Army would indeed place me in Vietnam. The recruiter was ecstatic. He tried to swear me in right there on the spot. Ever so careful, I stepped back to escape the salivating recruiter.

Why do I want to serve in Vietnam? I answer my own question *"With my skills, I can help war-wounded Americans."* What a heady response. I am a pediatric nurse that cares for seriously compromised children. Patients, those serving in Vietnam, are not children, they are combat-wounded men. I must have a strain of crazy in my DNA, as the incongruity of my thoughts only strengthens my resolve. I didn't realize that I was distancing myself from the death of my sister.

Until my conversation with the amputee patient, I am an Air National Guard nurse enjoying the moment. Relentless self-talk dogged me. I need something to reach down and pull me out of depression. *Maybe serving in the Army is just what I need.*

On our drive to work, I broach the subject of Vietnam with Carol, my apartment roomy. "I know you and I are asking for a domestic flight nurse assignment. What do you think about flying out of Saigon and serving in Vietnam?"

I put this question before her, as nonchalantly as asking her to place her head on a chopping-block.

I continued. "Did I share with you about the letter from the Air Force? They informed me they do not place the rank of lieutenants in Vietnam."

"It has been a couple of days since you talked about Vietnam," she replied.

Am I that obvious? I kept on talking,

"I've done some research and I will go to Vietnam with the Army Nurse Corps." I talk fast and said, "I understand, Carol, if you can't do this because of your dad."

She hesitates and said, "Did you think of this 'Vietnam' idea when you were with the active-duty flight nurses?"

I back-peddled to explain. "I know the timing seems crazy but let me share what happened on my last duty as a flight nurse." After I told Carol about the patient that was a double-leg amputee and needed only half of his litter, she said, "I hear you Judy. Let me think about it. You know my dad. I will think about it, is all I can promise."

A few days passed when I approach Carol again about Vietnam. "Have you been able to talk with your dad?"

"I've been checking," she replied. "There is a 'buddy system' where the Army stations friends together. If we can stay together, maybe Dad will be okay with me going to Vietnam."

So, on a whim, Carol and I submit a request to switch military services to the Army Nurse Corps.

I gave Carol's dad lots of space to grasp that his first-born wanted to serve in the Army, in a war, on the other side of the world. I realize that dads are used to sending sons, not daughters, to war.

My dad lives in Corpus Christi, a ten-hour drive from Oklahoma City. I drove across Texas, not to ask dad's permission, but to tell him my decision. Dad let me talk, then he said, "I served in WWII, Judy. You know this already. It was rough and, until now I gave no thought about you serving in the military. I want you to stay close by so nothing happens to you, but Donna wasn't protected; and she lived here with me. You are all I've got, Judy. So, be careful. There might be a time when you question your decision to go to war. Just know that you make me proud." This was heady stuff, coming from my Dad. He wanted to protect me. We both lived on the rough edges of our lives, as neither of us were protected from the grief of Donna's death.

Then it happened. It was a big day in my life when Carol and I raised our right hands and swore to serve the United States of America.

Lookout world, here I come.

With a knot in my stomach, I became the newest lieutenant in the United States Army Nurse Corps.

8

The Field Grade Officer

The uniforms they give us, they say are mighty fine,
but it would take Jane Mansfield to fill the front of mine!
Oh, I don't want no more of Army life!
Gee, Mom, I wanna go
But they won't let me go
Gee, Mom, I want to go home!
Sound off one, two, three, four . . .
Your right! Your right! Your right your

Boot Camp at Fort Sam Houston proved to be unsuccessful at teaching nurses to march, as more often than not an, "about face" ended with a few turning and the rest facing them and giggling. However, the field trip to Camp Bullis was a memory-maker (and we didn't even march).

We began with a ride to Camp Bullis, on benches, in the back of an Army duce-and-a-half-ton truck. I climbed off the truck to view acres of short, drab-green bushes and red, muddy ravines. We were decked-out in olive-green Army fatigues and baseball caps: we matched the scrub bushes.

"Women! You will spend the day with us here at Camp Bullis. It is our task to make stout soldiers out of everyone. At the end of the day, you will not even remember that once upon a time you were a civilian. The sergeant was cryptic. My learning curve had nowhere to go but up.

We were divided into platoons of six nurses; each platoon was given a compass and a map, with instructions to use the compass and locate the correct coordinates, and to map an azimuth and a back azimuth. We spent the day at Camp Bullis honing our map-reading skills, learned in classes at Fort Sam. The first platoon to accomplish this lofty goal was rewarded with a ride on a Huey helicopter. Using untested classroom techniques, we located true north on our map. Miracles did happen as we worked out the correct coordinates of the azimuth and back-azimuth. Our platoon hung on by a thread and, of course, didn't win the coveted prize. However, the pilot of the helicopter, on his free time, was a hustler.

He invited me on the date of my life. "Would you like a night ride, Lieutenant?" He need not ask twice as I was over the top with excitement. We agreed to meet that evening at Fort Sam's helipad.

I asked a nurse friend, "I've been invited to fly in a helicopter this evening. Do you want to go with me?"

"Oh, sweet," she said. "Thanks for the invite."

So, we two were off on a double date (double gal power). We both anticipated an interesting evening.

The pilot was a gentleman and took my date insurance in stride. After placing her behind the pilot seat and securing her straps tightly, he turned to me to ask, "Judy, do you want to come up with me to the flight deck?"

Giddy with excitement, I moved up to the "guts and glory" of the Huey. Speaking in an instructor tone, he handed me a set of earphones saying, "Place the headset on your ears. Good."

With an easy touch on the "stick," the long blades whoop, the nose dips, and the Heuy takes to the air. With the headset in place, I could hear him as clear as day.

"Now, Judy, see that ribbon of lights to your left? That's Interstate 35. We are high enough; just fly along with it. Our heading is north. Now you can take the stick."

In the span of a single day, I was looking for that pesky north again.

Evening traffic on Interstate 35 turns it into a milky-orange. I white-knuckle the stick and the chopper dips deep on its left side. To correct this near disaster, I jerked the stick the other direction, so the helicopter swings, like a grandfather clock, to the other side. My date, the suave heilo pilot, quickly corrals the itinerant machine, and as smooth as a feather, puts the skids back on the helipad.

I hoped my "date Insurance" was not thrown loose from the straps. No worry. When we landed, she came out of her bindings, wobbled off the chopper and called out to me, "Do not ask me to do anything with you. Ever. Forget I even know you."

And the LTC? We parted company at the helipad. Using my impeccable southern manners, I said, "Don't call me. I will call you. Goodbye. Thanks for the evening. Have a good life."

Life was merciful as the helicopter pilot and I did not cross paths again at Fort Sam. However, we almost crossed paths in

Vietnam in the 91st hospital mess hall. I must have been invisible, as the poised officer stared straight through me, and, not missing a beat, continued the conversation with his table mates.

To survive, I was not the naïve girl I was with the Air Guard. After the evening, when I viewed the lights of San Antonio from the vantage of a helicopter, I vowed to get wisdom, and to give a wide berth to Army Field Grade officers.

9

Monterey…California

Our first assignment after Basic Training, was at Ft. Ord, CA. in beautiful Monterey. I totally enjoy the last leg of the drive, and even the scary curves of Hwy One, as each 'switch-back' offers another spectacular view. Big Sur simply takes my breath away!

I am assigned to work the orthopedic ward and I'm primed to learn military nursing as, until now, I have only worked with children. Major Golden, the head of the ward is my superior officer. He works the day shift, leaving myself and a couple of lieutenants to cover the evening and the night shifts.

On the evening shift, when time allows, I do what I did, when I worked as a nurse-aide in college; I offer a back rub to patients confined to their bed. The one-on-one time spent with each soldier is rewarding, as they share about Vietnam and the firefight that brought them down. Some of the guys want to stay in the Army; get back to Vietnam and kill the damn VC. A couple of the men harbor a fear of being sent back to Vietnam. Most of them share a commonality; they want to return to what they knew before Uncle Sam rewrote their lives. I mused that,

"Their wounds are almost healed, however the deeper wound, inside, where no one can see, is raw."

Most of the patients are young, just out of high school. Until the 'old-man' came today from Travis Air Base, just north of Ft. Ord.

We share the same age, 25, however our age is all we have in common. It's hard to treat him like other patients, as he's different. He has been through sheer hell and is living on the backside of a nightmare. He's from Redondo Beach, about a four-hour drive south of Ft. Ord. This is his last stop before medical discharge from the Army. He said,

"My wife is on her way here. I called her when I got to Travis AB."

"Your wife? Does she know about your injury?"

"She knows, still I am a bit anxious, as this happened almost two months back. I still wake up and imagine it never happened, at least it didn't happen like this."

I see a handsome man sitting upright in the bed. We do a dance of sorts, as we both shy away from saying the word, *legs.*

A memory, ran through my mind, of when I served as a Flight Nurse and asked a patient,

"Are you comfortable? Do you want to be pulled up on the litter?" I'll not soon forget the flat tone of his voice, when he replied, 'I am comfortable like this, Ma'am as I have no legs!'

I continue with admitting procedures and note that, the ward is almost 'pin-drop quiet.'

"Are they listening to us talk or is it my imagination? This is an

open ward and until now, it didn't register; there were no curtains to shield curious eyes."

I turn to walk away when I almost bump into a visitor. I start to ask her if I could help, when she stood at the foot of his bed and stared.

There were no hugs, there were no kisses, she did not even tell him hello; they just looked at each other as though they were the only people in the room.

She found her voice and said,

"Get your things together. You're getting out of here. I cleared it with the hospital and have secured a room for us!"

She is not a 'looker,' no-problem, as without a doubt, she loves her man: a fact that offers him strength for the journey, as her acceptance gives him life.

Quiet-on-the-ward-weights-heavy. When a couple of patients began a slow clap that moves like a ripple, until the entire ward claps for her. No words! Her acceptance of him shouts loud,

I love this man! No legs! Be damn!

10

Bing Cherries

I am on duty at midnight. and the ward is stirring. A patient at the end of the ward has a medicine due. I enter the ward, and the door closes behind me. I stand still to let my eyes adjust to the darkness, then walk on squishy objects strewed across the floor. I give the patient his med, when something lands on the floor near my feet. I pick up the object. 'It is a pillowcase tied in a knot.' I toss it back in the direction that it came.

"Hey! What's that?" booms a voice in the dark.

"Your pillowcase!" I reply.

"Why didn't someone tell us the Lieutenant is in here?"

Their game is up. In the cave-like dark, I walk to the end of the ward and turn on the lights. The entire floor, as well as their sheets and pillowcases, are littered with, the purple juice of plump, dark-red Bing cherries! I ask a patient to sweep up the mess when he grumbles,

"Ma'am, I'm not part of this mess! I had nothing to do with their fight! A visitor brought a boat-load of cherries and after the visitors left, the fight was on! They (pointing to the guys across the aisle) threw cherries until they ran out, then they knotted their pillowcases and threw them across the aisle! Didn't you know Ma'am that you broke up a war between the beds!"

"I apologize soldier. But there are but a few of you-guys that walk without crutches."

Come morning, I share with Major Golden, the ward head nurse, about the cherry-fight, then I consider it a closed subject. When I come on duty that night, a man wearing standard hospital light blue pajamas meets me at the nurses desk. He is MSsgt. Howard and holds the rank, of a Non-Commissioned Officer patient on the ward.

He corners me, and in a dogmatic tone says, "Lieutenant, I am here to tell you there will be no problems like that ruckus that happened last night."

I offer him due honor, as were he wearing his uniform (instead of the traditional hospital blue pajamas) his chest would bear a rack of well-earned medals.

"You mean the cherry fight, Sergeant?"

"Yeah! The cherry fight. That's what I'm talking about. The cherry fight!"

Considering his rank and his age, I may be talking to a Korean Veteran. I honor the NCO rank and step back to give him space to correct me. Then my thoughts catch up with me, and I stretch-tall (60' inches tall) to share a litany of details about the patients, until now, I didn't realize I knew.

"I know what is important about the patients; I know their

names, and the fire-fight in Vietnam that wounded them and took them down. I even know about their Bud that did-not-live. I know how they feel about the Army. I know where they are from and where they plan to go when they are discharged."

I paused to take a breath when the MSsgt interjected, "Well, I know discipline; and I know the lack of discipline when I see it."

His last statement irritated me.

"Allow me to talk, Sir, as I don't want to be misunderstood. Most of the men who were part of the 'cherry fight' last night have not been outdoors since the firefight in Vietnam that landed them in a hospital. If all they do to upset protocol is a 'cherry-fight,' then I am okay with it!" I turned away to show the MSsgt. that this 'conversation' was ended.

I do not understand the military institution that pulsates through the MSsgt's veins. The Army has a steep learning curve and I better suck it in, if I am going to survive the next two years!

11

Ft. Ord and Bill Greiner

One would think the guys are cheering a race. No! It's Bill. They are screaming about one of my favorite patients. Bills left leg is stabilized with a thin wire in a Balkan Frame. If he falls; then the bone growth will be destroyed!

The boisterous cheers continue,

"Just a little more! Almost, Bill!"

"Bill, you have been on your back for months," I scold him. "Regrowth of the femur takes time."

You roll your 'doll' eyes at me and want 'me' to understand?

"I haven't touched the floor in a long time, Lt.," you tell me.

Youth, in this man's Army, offers no time as they barge at breakneck speed into the next season of their lives. In the dark of night, when the guys are sleeping, I pull up a chair next to your bed and listen to you talk.

"We went to Nam, courtesy of the draft board, that 'just

ate-us-up.' We didn't have the escape-route of the wealthy and the privilege. Those well-do-to dads kept their boy in school. I know that's true," you say.

Your stories were hard to hear; you talked about sloshing through rice paddies with your platoon, and walking neck-line in muddy rivers, with your arms held tight over your head to protect the radio.

"Gotta hold up the radio. Gotta keep her dry," you explain.

You go on to say, "Nothing fooled me, not even for a minute. I walked alongside the Cpt. with my radio and sent his messages. We called down fire from the fighter planes up high. They were just a dot in the sky. Those fly-guys got it made; they dropped that ammo, peeled off and flew back from wherever they come from. No dirt under their nails. No Ma'am."

You keep on talking,

"Being the radioman, I knew everything before it happened. The hardest call to put through, was to bring in Dust-Off choppers, to come take our wounded out. We loaded our guys on the chopper, real fast, to get that Huey back in the air. We cheated the NVA (North Vietnamese Army) the precious minutes needed, to get a good read on the chopper and shoot it down. The bodies; we would hold off and pile them on last. First, we loaded the wounded, then we loaded our heroes: our men whose-life-was-plum-sucked-out-of-them."

You pause; I sat quiet and heard your tears.

"Can't say nothing good about being radio-man, if it was sad, then my heart held the 'sad' a bit longer than the rest of the troops did. That's all. I was good at imitating the Cpt.'s orders. My voice just carried better, so I'd repeat the orders just like they rolled off his tongue."

Maybe you shared more than intended. I will never know as you changed the subject and talked about the plus of serving in the boonies.

"We had a star show every night, it was real pretty, but the stars were the only thing pretty. As I didn't know from sundown to sunup if it would be my last. I taught myself to breathe real shallow. I'm ashamed to say this, but I was so scared that some nights, I wet my pants. Those inky black nights put together threating shapes that messed with my mind. I'd creep-around just hoping to be alive when the sun clawed her way above the rice patties and slipped to light the world with another day."

"On dark nights, I was extra careful to not 'toke-a-smoke.' I couldn't even draw in a quick drag as I feared Charlie would get a read on a cigarette. I knew that the lives of my Buds depended on my being sober. Occasional flares from out of nowhere, made for a pretty burst' that lit up the sky. I knew right quick that it wasn't the Cong trying to take my life. Nope! I'd been a fearing' a bush or a tree."

I sat quiet, listening to you talk, and am amazed with the comraderie you have for those wounded in your platoon. War melted your heart with the black person in the platoon. No matter, "he bleeds red and he is part of me."

"I was careful not to shoot one of our own. Happen you know, when there was no moon and the dark didn't settle down to dim shadows. Why, some nights, it was so dark, I could barely see my hand right in front of my face. I've heard about troops going down in 'friendly-fire' Noises bother me anyway, and I try to keep pace with my listening skills. I know the difference in your shoes and Major Goldens shoes. And, even with my eyes shut, I know when you walk onto the ward."

His revelation suggested a tease.

"Not everyone wears 'White Shoulder' perfume?" I asked.

"I should say!" you are quick to reply. "Don't need to be in this man's Army if a guy wears girl perfume!"

I left your bedside and did a quiet walk-a-bout around the ward. It was late, and my ears were rewarded with the rhythmic sounds of men sleeping.

I've listened to the news and have heard the war protestors. Are they proud to be an American? I love my country; I salute our flag and place my hand over my heart to pledge allegiance. Surely, these protesting, don't desecrate our flag, the Stars and Stripes is their flag too. And WWI and WWII suffered more deaths and casualties than Vietnam. Would I recognize a protestor, should I meet one? Long, stringy, oily hair, maybe. This person screaming for the right to not fight in Vietnam could well be the rich mans' kid. I just don't understand their way of loving our country.

Do they not know that most of the men serving in Vietnam did not have a choice? Like their dads, they went where Uncle Sam sent them…and many of the young soldiers came back home zipped in a body bag.

12

Home Sweet Home

I sat beside a window seat on the flight to Vietnam and made restroom trips when the guy-passengers were dozing. I hid my gender amongst a plane of men. Our duffel bags were tossed onto large trucks when a couple of bags rolled off one truck. Out of the opening, of one of the bags, spilled a girly item. I almost heard them twist their necks like doll heads as the guys turn in unison to look at me. I grab the bag, push my jamie back in, pull the cord tight and calmly ask the guy next to me,

"Would you mind tossing my bag back on the truck?"

I board a drab Army green bus; with the windows covered with a heavy cyclone fence material. I am sitting behind the driver, when a Ssgt. steps into the bus and yells,

"Attention! This bus takes you to Long Binh. The windows are covered anti-grenade screens, for your protection!"

The military does not want the replacement soldiers' dead. Sweet!

I can do this.
I am well qualified to serve in Vietnam.
I am an R.N. three years post grad.
I graduated from the Air Force aeronautical nurse medical program.
I trained to care for war wounded at the renown Ft. Sam Houston nurse program.
I worked for six months with Vietnam wounded at Ft. Ord.
Can I do this?

I spent my first night in Vietnam in a trailer; positioned on top of a barren hill, guarded by a soldier brandishing an M16 rifle. The best part about the trailer; it's air-conditioned! Been awhile since I've slept, so without fanfare, I drift off to sleep. When a loud explosion wakens me. I sit upright and exclaim,

"We are under attack, and we just got here!"

The door shakes and the gate-guard shouts,

"An ammo-dump blew-up, there is nothing to worry 'bout, Ladies. Sleep well."

An ammo-dump. What is an ammo-dump? I'm exhausted; the 'ammo-dump' explosion spilled an enormous amount of adrenalin in my body and the guard tells me to "sleep well?"

Night rolls into day. Long Bien is a huge base, so with the help of a fold-up map, I locate a mess hall for breakfast. I am rejuvenated and ready to meet the day. Using a map, I locate the Medical Processing building. I enter the room to see a couple of women, *dressed in fatigues*. It takes me back to Camp Bullis when the drab-green of our Army fatigues blended with murky-green scrub trees. No trees here, I muse.

I do not 'blend' well. I am wearing the summer female Army Cord

uniform, a skirt with a fitted short-sleeve top. I make a note, *"get-out-of-this-girl-garb-and-into fatigues."*

The MSG. greets me, picks up a thin black rod, and turns to a map that covers the length of the wall. He goes on to say,

"This is your hospital Lieutenant, in II Corps, where you will spend the next year. Get there any way you can. Hitchhike if you must, just report to duty ASAP."

"Hitchhike." Surely, he did not intend for me to raise my thumb on the roads in Vietnam. He also left it up to me to *"get-to-your-hospital-anyway-you-can."*

I step closer to get a better look of Vietnam. The country appears to be penned in 'code' as the places are all written in Vietnamese. Prior to Army, I am Air Force, where I learned to catch a hop (aircraft going my way) to reach a destination. I snag a ride in a jeep-convertible (a jeep with no top…I thought it was a small convertible) and am dropped off in front of a building near the flight line. The man at the desk can't help but smell me coming; the woman walking toward his desk, wearing an odiferous, crumpled girl-Army uniform. He intended the smell of me to be away from his desk, as I am destined to take the next helicopter headed to the 91st Evacuation Hospital. I'm reluctant to ride in the helicopter; as a memory of the night ride over Interstate 35, flashes through me clear as a bell, I can still hear the voice of the LtCol.

"Now Judy, see that ribbon of lights to your left? That's I-35. We are high enough, just fly along with it. Our heading is north. Now you can take the stick." I'm holding the stick! The helicopter almost crashed because, I-was-holding-the-stick!"

I tremble and back away, when the guy at the door of the machine reaches out to catch my duffel bag.

"Get on Judy. My self-talk tries to calm my soul. Just do not go near the 'flying' part of the helicopter."

No one knew that I prefer to go by road to my assignment when he reached out and pulled me into the chopper. My regulation shoes (black pumps (part of the summer uniform) are a definite handicap. I dare not remove them, as they have a vice grip on my swollen feet. My feet were not the only part of me that needed attention as I felt the urge to vomit, at just the thought of getting in the helicopter. Stop it Judy… I berated myself, *"people back home at the State Fair would stand in line and pay good money to ride in a helicopter.*

The door-guy straps me in tight and off we go. I am glad the straps over my torso are sturdy, as the helicopter flew with both doors open with the gunner hunched at the door. The wind blew hard and he didn't even flinch as he grips an M16 to monitor the air between us and the treetops. I didn't have time to puke as the helicopter kicked up a flurry of dust and set the Huey down, close to the buildings with a 'larger-than-life' Red Cross on the top. I push back the nasty taste of bile in my throat and head toward the never-closed-open door when a hand pushed my head down hard!

The guy at the door screams above the drone of the helicopter, "Them blades wo-a-cut your head off, Ma'am. This be your home for a year. Just 'keep your head down' and you'll be all right."

13

Horny

My mind does a two-step. As the soldier's response caught me off guard, an innate sixth sense cautioned me to maintain eye contact with him. I stretched my sixty-inch frame, squared my shoulders and locked eyes with the six-foot man towering over me. *He will not best me!*

He leaned over the nurse's desk and, with a poker-straight face said, "But Lieutenant, it's been a long time!"

"Let me get this straight," I replied. "It's dark as sin outside (a southern colloquial saying) and you want to go to Phu Hiep village?"

"Yes, Ma'am," replied the person dressed in blue hospital pajamas, not batting an eye.

Army Boot Camp did not prepare me for this conversation. With six weeks in-country, I am a newbie. Even so, I will not be messed with.

I asked, "What do you think this hospital is, soldier, a brothel?" *This soldier has more than his share of testosterone fueling his blood.*

I take a step back to let my question settle, then I keep talking. "The wards' of the 91st border an area of mined sand. Should you manage to not trigger a bomb, then when you are in the village, you will be rolled for your money. It's too dangerous, Private."

With my lips thin and tight, I went on to say, "I am responsible for your safety. Going to the village is ludicrous!"

In exasperation and with more bravado than I feel, I told him, "I have work to do on the Vietnamese ward. This conversation is over."

The night was young and several of the Vietnamese patients need their dressings changed. However, try as I may, I could not shake the cloud hovering over me. I listened to my gut and returned to the GI ward. When the subtle noises on the ward settled down to a roaring silence. 'I was on center stage.' The man of the hour is in his bed, with a scratchy army-green wool blanket pulled up around his shoulders.

I asked, "Going to bed early, soldier?"

"Yes, ma'am," he replied as he turned his head away from me.

"You're covered with blankets? Do you have a chill?" I asked.

"No, ma'am," he said, with his head still turned away from me.

My voice, dripped with sarcasm when I said, "Here, let me see if your skin is warm."

I reached out to pull the Army blanket away from his face. "Your fatigues. You are wearing your fatigues. You're not even wearing hospital pajamas!"

I am more upset by the minute. He doesn't resist me when I pull the blanket away from his torso. "And you're wearing your boots. I know, you'll tell me you are Infantry, and as Infantry you never part with your boots."

I did not give him a sliver of a minute to answer, when I said, "Sit up, Soldier. All the way up." My voice subconsciously snapped to an officer-command tone. "Take off your boots."

He sat up, slung his gangly legs over the edge of the bed, bent over and pulled off one boot at a time.

"Now, give them to me."

"But, Lieutenant. Oh, Ma'am, not my boots! These are MY boots!" he replied, as though he was parting with a revered treasure.

"Give me your boots!" The sternness in my voice startled even me.

One boot at a time, the Sky Soldier of the honored Airborne 173rd Infantry, handed me the most essential part of his uniform, his boots. I carried his odiferous boots to the Vietnamese ward and placed them under the nurses' desk.

I was glad that the Vietnamese patients did not try to converse with me, as I was angry to the point that I didn't trust myself to talk. I only knew three to four Vietnamese words anyway. I offered a quick smile and finished their final dressings.

When a patient from the GI ward (next door) interrupted my thoughts.

"Ma'am, we guys thought you otter' know that Private Spearman is gone."

"Gone? Gone where?"

"He went to the village, Ma'am. He's been gone a long time, and we's worried 'bout 'em."

"But, but . . . I have his boots. Did you give him 'your' boots?"

"No, Ma'am, I wouldn't do that," he replied.

"You mean he went to the village barefoot?"

The events of the night morphed into the inconceivable. I readily admitted to being the weak link in the pecking order of command, as the NCOIC (Non-Commission Officer in Charge) bears ultimate responsibility for the safety and well-being of our GI patients. I berate my judgment and realize I should have called the NCOIC at the git-go. When the sergeant knows the story, the worst-case scenario could happen; that my patient would be court martialed.

Think military, Judy, as you may also be court martialed!

With this pessimistic drama in mind, I asked our corpsman to take a message to Sergeant Haverly. The corpsman was still on the ward when, the "man of the hour" ambled out of the dark night on to the ward. His head hung down, as though he was analyzing every step. And he is barefoot.

He avoids making eye contact with me and even begins to apologize. I stop him mid-sentence and dump on him the fear and frustration he had created for me.

"Save your breath, Sky Soldier," I told him. "You are a damn shame to the 173rd Airborne Infantry. They taught you to jump out of an airplane. But they failed to teach you one iota of plain old' common sense. Every breath your mother takes is a prayer that you will survive this bloody war and come back to her safe and sound!"

14

Fragging

Breakfast was served on the ward to patients unable to go to the mess-hall. Our newest admission, MSsgt. Bumm came to us a few hours ago, from Emergency. His hands were severely burned, and he needed help to eat.

I overheard two of our ambulatory patients arguing, "The hell I will, " said one guy under his breath. "Well, I refuse!"

I'm confused, as the person they refuse to help was a stranger to them. They are not even in the same Division as MSsgt. Bumm. Word of the new patient slid like quick silver, you know it's there, but it's impossible to hold. I diffused the argument between my ambulatory patients and told them, "you guys break it up and go on to the mess-hall."

I visited with the MSsgt. while I fed him his breakfast, and asked, "What happened that your hands burned?"

"Don't wanna talk about it. Thanks for helping me. Why I can't even get a swallow of water, and I am a MSsgt! I don't deserve this!"

I mused how the tables are turned, as I left the MSsgt. to his mumblings. My ward corpsmen even refused to care for the him. So, my last resort was to go to the top for help. I walked to the Administrators Office to talk with Major Lackey, a proud 'lifer' who enjoys exerting his position over we low-life Lieutenants.

"Major Lackey, good morning. I have a situation brewing and need your help." (I worded this to make the Major feel indispensable)

"What brings you here, Lt?"

I explained, "The GI ward admitted a patient, MSsgt. Bumm, early this morning. Both his hands are wrapped in dressings. The problem stems with the GI patients, as they refused to help the man. They won't even help him eat and I'm sure that helping him with his toilet is out of the question. I heard the guys talking about 'fragging' and in the same breath almost cursing the MSsgt.' very existence."

Major Lackey leaned back and rocked in his chair, then replied, "I am aware of this patient, Lt., and I am also aware of how he was injured. Seems he was not liked by the men under him. Maybe he showed poor judgement and men under him died when he sent them into battle. I just shared the worse possible scenario, so don't take it as truth. Our patient, MSsgt. Bumm, juggled a live grenade hand-to-hand when he was sleeping. The grenade went off and his fingers are burned, almost to the bone. The Pvts. went for a kill and failed."

"But," I replied, "the patients who refused to help him are not even in the same unit, or even the same Division as MSsgt. Bumm. Why, he's been on the ward only a few hours; you relate, the reason his hands are burned, what I don't understand is, how do my GI patients know this and why did they refuse to help him?"

Major Lackey looked away then reluctantly shared, "it's lonely at the top, and men under our command become agitated. Put alcohol and pot together and the Pvts' become destroyers. This is how I understand what's happened. I will have the MSsgt. moved to ICU where his daily care will not be left to other patients. Thanks, for stopping by."

Major Lackey blamed the MSsgt.'s injury on a mixture of pot and alcohol. I don't agree with him, as I consider that MSsgt. Bumm probably didn't treat the soldiers under him fairly. My questions were not answered, however the tension in the room was palpable. Major Lackey was not well liked by lowly Lieutenants, still I would not allow harming him to weigh on my conscience.

Like a parade, a scene ran through my mind of a patient in ICU, an Army Cpt. who lost his arm. He was livid with anger and kept mumbling, "I'm career Army, so, what happens to me now? My arm is gone, and I can never get it back and this will follow me. I'll be shipped out to some old-folk-veteran place where I will rot-till-I-die!" The Cpt. talked a lot, but not the kind of talk that encourages conversation. He was evacuated to Japan the next day. We nurses and the corpsmen kept quiet with our thoughts. Looking back, the Cpt. that lost an arm, was also the recipient of 'fragging' He survived a life, career changing injury and he also didn't die. Maybe the ones that perpetrated the injuries didn't want killing an American to weigh on their conscience.

I walked back to the ward and the MSsgt was transferred to ICU where he enjoyed special care. End of story, sort of. The next day, I talked to the two guys about their refusal to feed MSsgt. Bumm. "But, how did you know?" I asked, "he was only here for a few hours?"

"We don't need details and our guess was 'spot-on'! Combat has done a number on us Ma'am. The rest of our days, we'll live in the shadow of Nam.' It's a high learnin' curve and many of our Buds lost their lives. The MSsgt. must not have treated the Pvts. and all under him with plain-ole-decency."

I could hear Major Lackey, like I was standing in front of him, "I am aware of this patient Lt. and I am also aware how he was injured. Seems he was not liked by the enlisted men under him. Maybe his judgement was lacking, and men under him died when he sent them into battle."

I listen as the young soldiers share, "Covering for your 'Bud' is the best way to get out of this hell-hole alive. About the men over us? It's a judgment call, Ma'am, and it don't take long to know which Non-Coms and Officers give a shit if we live or die."

15

Susie

Screams run ramshod over my dreams. Wake up! Stop screaming! I am awake and I am not screaming. The nightmare is only louder. I roll over only to realize the screams came from outside. It's a girl screaming. Is a guy hurting her? No, this is a scream of pain that comes from the bottom of her soul!

I ran out of the end of our hooch to find Susie screaming uncontrollably. She is alone. Susie, Susie! By now several nurses in pajamas gathered around her. She pushed us away only to scream louder!

"Don't you know? I am here in this hell-hole so he will not be drafted! My brother! My brother! He is here now in this godforsaken country.... I volunteered and I joined the Army just to keep...my...brother...out of Nam!"

"But you know he can't be drafted Susie, as only one family member can be drafted. Did he lie to the draft board? Did he not tell them that his sister is serving in Vietnam?"

"He didn't lie! He did not lie! He joined! He joined the fucking marines!"

Susie pushed us away and kept on crying and screaming. When our Chief Nurse showed up she put her arms around Susie and walked her to Emergency Receiving.

I am back in my room but getting to sleep is crazy. I finally gave up. I needed not to be alone. I joined a couple of nurses that also couldn't sleep. I hurt for Susie, as she is a cheerful, well-put-together gal.

Volunteering to serve in Vietnam just to keep your brother safe at home is what being a big sister is all about.

16

The Ward

"Ladies, I do not care where you go, or what you do on your free time. You will show up for duty when your name is on the roster and you-will-not-be-sunburned!"

Humidity rules tonight and the collar of my fatigues chaffs against my neck. It was too hot to sleep today so, I went to the beach and slept. And I have a sun burn.

"You should have an easy shift" Lynn, the day nurse says, "See you in the morning. I hope tonight goes smoothly. Remember that 'Victor Charlie' owns the night."

I walked next door, to the GI ward, when I heard my corpsman, Pvt. Shann, tell the guy going off duty to be on time in the morning. Pvt. Shann is a good worker. Life is not easy for him, as he is the only black person working the ward. We work together a couple of twelves a week, and over time he loosens up and lets me into his world. Tonight, all the light bulbs along the open walkway, from the wards to the mess hall are busted. I looked at the broken bulbs and Pvt. Shann's name popped into my thoughts.

I have little time for cultured conversation, so I outright asked Pvt. Shann, "The lights along the corridor are busted. No comment, Pvt.?"

"Don't hab' nuttin' to say, Ma'am."

"Did you break them Pvt. Shann?"

"I's had it! I jes' angry!" he explodes.

"You don't seem upset," I reply, trying to keep him from shutting me out of his thoughts.

"Nope, not angry 'wid' you Ma'am. It's da-Ssgt. He rides me. He wons' to section-eight me outta da Army!"

"Where're you from Pvt.?"

"Alabama Ma'am. I's drafted. It shows, don't it? I's jes' two mons' left, den I be-a-free man!"

I share with him,

"The military's a fast learning curve for me. Can you put up with the Ssgt. for two more months?" I asked. "I wouldn't expect him to let up, and God knows, as a lowly Lt. I can't stand up for you!" Wisdom just slipped off my tongue, "Why, you're young and the rest your life hangs on an honorable discharge. Am I making sense Pvt.?" I slow down, so he doesn't confuse this talk with a lecture. "Pvt. didn't you spend six months in the Field?"

He replied, "Yes Ma'am. I didn't sign-on as a medic. I's be da' nex medic, wen our, medic jes' died. And I likes heppin' our guys, so da' how I be here. We work hab' da' year in da' field and da' rest, I be alive an I works witchu, in da' hospital. Being black, I knows bout' how de Army uses us. Can't do nothin bout it tho. So I's be quiet and jes humps my pack."

"Been a rough year, for you Pvt. Shann. Just think of the learning that's come your way!" I offer him a sincere compliment. "Why, you can easily work in a hospital back-home!"

"Yes Ma'mn." He muttered quietly, "I jes' hab' sixty mo' days. I jes' gotta keep my thot's quiet, inside. It 'heps me to jes' talk a bit."

"Pvt. Shann, you are what? 18 or 19 years old?"

"I's nineteen, Ma'am."

"Then you have bragging' rights, as you served in the '68 'Tet' offensive."

"Yes Ma'am… Come night-time, selong I didn't talk, others didn't seem to cares bout' de color my skin. Sum nights I be so scared I'd piss on myself. Nites I pulled guard duty, I feared falling in de 'Punji Pits' the Cong made. If youse falls in one, deys pits, filled wit sharp bamboo stick, dat dey done smeared wit der own shit. Step in de Punji Pit! Youse for sure be outta action…mites loose yore leg!"

In a small way, maybe I can touch Pvt. Shann's world. He may exceed his wildest dreams and someday be an honorable leader in his community. Maybe, this is the reason I am in Vietnam? I want him to know that, the Ssgt may give him trouble, but this nurse has confidence in him

"Jim Crow Laws…as a boy, took your thoughts, and the thoughts of your mother. Your being black must of…

"Dem Jim Crow laws are older dan me. Dem rules our life… for sure, sometimes I's feel like, de laws got an ugly hand round my neck. De laws been ruling southern blacks for a long time. Been only sum' years dat blacks can vote. I lives in a small town. Sometimes I be safer here wit youse whites in Nam, dan livin bac in Bama.' My Mamma done vots for de first time in her life and she be forty! She fussed about votin, she says, "de vote wus writtin wit so many words. It jes kept de blacks mixed up, and side's dat, wasn't no blacks to vote for! But my Momma, she do pray! Oh yes! My Momma do pray!"

"The mothers of everyone here in Vietnam prays, Pvt. Shann, of this you can be sure. Oh yes! You can bank on this Pvt."

17

Merry Christmas, Mom and Dad

There seems to be no end to the flow of combat casualties. Men, America's best: Uncle Sam lists you as men, your mother calls you, her boy.

Well-oiled teams work furtively, against the clock, as the minutes of your lives slip away. To me you are not part of a mass casualty, to a man, you are special. I do not remember your name, still, when I close my eyes, I see your bed on the ward. Your left leg, despite aggressive measures to save it, is mutilated. I try to brace you for the shock of an amputation. When I hear myself saying, "In the States there is an Army Hospital in Colorado where they take you up to the mountain and the ski-patrol teach you to ski with one leg. Do you ski soldier?"

No sooner do the words leave my mouth when I swallow hard and say a one-liner to God and confess that I need to keep my mouth shut.

You ignore my thoughtless question to ask, "Lt. will you help me write a letter to my folks?"

God grants me to be part of a pivotal moment when you confide with me, a piece of your heart. Write your family? I search for paper; any piece of paper will do; as I don't want anything to sully your confidence in me. Pen in hand, I speak to my racing heart and sit down at your bedside to say, "Okay, I am ready. What do you want the letter to say?"

"Dear Mom and Dad,

I am out of action for a while, but I'm gonna be okay."

Our eyes connect, and in a whisper voice I ask, "Do you want to tell them about your injuries?"

My question hovers over the sultry air surrounding your bed, now we are both dancing around the word, *leg* when my thoughts go to your mother. I didn't think about your father, I thought about your mother: the woman who birthed you, watched you grow into a man and then sent you off to war.

In a pensive moment, with a wrinkled forehead, you consider your options, "Nah."

You answer, with an indifference that contrasts the gravity of the conversation. Then you ask, "It's near Christmas isn't it? I don't want to spoil their Christmas. Just tell them I'm okay, I love them, and I hope they have a Merry Christmas."

18

Welcome to MARS

The 'hospital jeep' boasts a new coat of paint, that covers the original designated unit number on the bumper. Without the tell-tail number, the search for the missing jeep is over before it begins. The mysterious jeep came to us without an ignition key. Not a problem as the starter is hotwired.

"Judy, will you take me to the MARS Station (Military Air Radio Station) at Tuy Hoa? I need to call my husband in Kansas. I hate to ask but if I call much later, he will be asleep."

I gave my nurse friend my, "I-just-need-sleep" look. She doesn't read my thoughts, and she goes on to say,

"I know you are wondering if anyone else could help, but seriously I don't want to be caught dead near the Doc's hooches and you're the only nurse that drives the Jeep."

I didn't inquire about the rush to call her husband, as it had to be urgent. My first thought is, I have worked all night, and she trusts me, to drive her to the Air Base? "Okay, Rosie, just let me change out of my fatigues."

"You look okay," she answered, "Can you come right now? I am hoping everyone will be on duty and the station will have a good line."

"Okay, Rosie," the urgency in her voice pushes sleep back. I ask, "Let's find the jeep. Have you seen it this morning?"

"No, but it's early, so I just hope you can get the key and the jeep is available."

"Don't need a key, just need the jeep, as it's hot-wired."

Simply explained; to start the jeep, reach your right hand down just under the dash, where two thingies dangle, grab them and put them together so they touch, push the heel of your right foot on the gas pedal, and stretch the ball of your right foot hard on the starter (the knob on the floor board of the jeep) Then, with your left foot, push in the pedal (it is near the door) and milk it a little and tahdah! The engine starts!

Entering Tuy Hoa Base is easy, as round-eyed gals are always welcome. I parked the jeep on a bit of sand, and we went inside. The station is one part of a trailer, with a bench to accommodate persons waiting to place a call. Best of all, the MARS station had air-conditioning!

The best way to explain a MARS station goes like this;

It is a way for the military service to place calls to the States. The beam from the MARS station bounces off a satellite and is picked up by a ham-radio operator in the States. The Ham operator picks up the call and places it to the number in the States.

Rosie, with a flustered face, anxiously awaits her turn, "It shouldn't be too long, Ma'am." The operator assures her.

Fatigue catches up with me. I lean against the wall to relax, when an Air Force MP enters the station.

He approached me, to ask, "Ma'am, are you the driver of the Army jeep?"

I nodded yes.

"Will you step outside with me, please."

I followed the MP out the door when he asked,

"Is this your jeep?"

"I drove it to the base, if that's what you want to know," I replied.

I am not about to offer any information about the 91st Hospital's mysterious acquisition of me, driving a stolen military vehicle.

"Well, you are illegally parked. Just show me your driver's license."

"My driver's license. You want to see my driver's license?"

"Yes Ma'am."

"I have a Texas license. But I didn't bring it with me." I muse that the Airman takes his job seriously.

"No, Ma'am, your 'military driver's license' I need to see your military license, as you are illegally parked."

"Sir, I do not have a military license."

My heart is pounding with dread. If I get a ticket, I will be remembered as the nurse-who-lost-the-hospital-jeep.

"How did you come to drive this jeep without a military license?"

I lied when I said, "It is assigned to our hospital and I don't have a special license to drive it. I didn't know I needed one."

Now I am wide awake at the thought of being 'the nurse that lost our 91st Hospital jeep!'

The MP continues on with his military rant, "Ma'am just park the jeep over there," he says, pointing to an obvious parking area on the asphalt, "and I will forget to remember that we ever met!"

Back in the MARS trailer, I sit in the air-conditioned trailer and exhale. I came close to the 'Air Force Military-Law' knowing the truth about the pilfered jeep! I recovered from the 'parking-crisis' when I heard Rosie holler into the microphone,

"Honey, I'm pregnant!"

The room goes 'pin-drop-quiet' in a magical moment of awe. As everyone in the MARS station turned to look at Rosie. We shared the exact moment-when-her husband learns-that-he-will-be-a-father.

"Honey, I'm pregnant!" Rosie hollered again into the phone.

The MARS operator, fusses over Rosie, like she's in labor. He went on to say, "Ma'am, your voice is soft, and it doesn't carry over, to the States. Is it okay for me to relay the message to your husband?"

Rosie nods, while trying to hold back tears that stream down her face.

The Airman cleared his throat and in his highest-pitch-male voice, hollered into the phone, "Honey. I'm pregnant! OVER!" His voice was met with silence. Then he hollered again, "Honey, I'm pregnant!"

Silence, like the line was dead; then it crackles to life. We were all primed to hear Rosie's husband's voice when a deep-base voice replies,

"This is Guam receiving. Your message is without a doubt the best ruse we've heard all day! You guys will try anything to get out of Vietnam!" I sweat bullets, coming so close to losing the 91st jeep. I drove Rosie back to our compound and vowed never to drive a jeep again!

19

A Mystery

My mind raced ninety miles an hour! I need to examine her! How? She is anxious to the point of hysteria. Think Judy! I know! I will wash her, with the guise of changing the sheets, then I'll have a good look at her backside.

I introduce myself. "I'm Lt. Crausbay. I am your nurse tonight. Are you in pain?"

She looked at me and just stared. I point to her leg and use one of the few Vietnamese words in my repertoire, "Dow?"

She shook her head no. I'm encouraged, so I go for broke and ask her, "Can I look at your leg?"

She stuck her leg out from the sheet. The dressing is bloody. On instinct, I reach down to pull her sheet back, when we engage in a bit of tug-of-war and the sheet falls to the floor. The dressing on her leg wound, is not near as bloody as is her bottom sheet!

I move quickly as time does not stand still. There is no running water on the ward. *(We wash our hands in a basin of dilute betadine and rinse them in a basin of water.)* I run to the communal shower, fill a basin with water and am back at her bedside.

She turns over to let me wash her backside. There is no break in her skin, not even a bruise! I think out loud,

"I hoped this menial task allows me into her world."

I need our Vietnamese interpreter. I chide myself (why didn't I send for him when this started?). I locate my corpsman on the GI ward next door to ask, "Pvt Shann, I need Frenchy to interpret. I realize it's late. I have no idea as to his where-a-bouts."

While waiting on Pvt. Shann, I visit with several of our GI patients and note which ones need their wounds assessed and dressings changed.

Pvt. Shann returns with our interpreter; Frenchy is a handsome French looking Vietnamese teen-ager.

"Good evening Frenchy, I'm glad you're here!" My eyes focus on his face when I say, "I-need-your-help."

Our GI patients are all ears, as they know something's going down on the ward next door. Frenchy and I walk to the Vietnamese ward when I ask,

"I need to know if the girl in bed seventeen has started her monthly period." A blank stare spread across his face.

"You know!" I keep talking, "the monthly bleeding that happens to women! If she says this has never happened to her, then tell her she will bleed a few days each month."

Even though I am new 'in-country' I should know better than to ask a Vietnamese male, a teen-ager at that, to engage in an intimate conversation with a young female! Our gregarious interpreter stared at the floor and his face lost all its bluster! I press on, "Frenchy! Listen to me, can you talk to her?"

"I help you Ma'am. I feel not good."

"I apologize for asking this of you, but we do not have a lady interpreter."

He straightened his back and said, "Okay, I do this, I do-this-for-you."

Standing at the foot of the girl's bed I listen to Frenchy visit with my patient, speaking to her in the familiar Vietnamese singsong nasal lilt. Then his voice changed, to a matter-of-fact tone, as if lecturing her. He stops talking, turned and ran off the ward.

I need to talk with him, so I put, 'Visit with Frenchy' on a mental list of tasks to do when the patients are settled in for the night.

I go next door to the GI ward when Pvt. Shann, and I trade places. Even though I am tired, just visiting with our GI patients, rejuvenates my spirit. Most of the GI's will go back to the 'field' when their wounds heal. Right now; they can shower, sleep on a mattress between clean sheets, and write home to their mother to let her know that her son is safe. I complete the tasks on the GI ward and left them talking quietly amongst themselves.

My focus is on the Vietnamese ward, specifically the girl in bed seventeen. I walk to her bed and say, hello. When I notice that her color has changed. She seems pale. Is she pale, or is my mind messing with me? I choose my words and ask, "dow?" (pain) I have almost exhausted my grasp of their language. Her head nods yes. I'm encouraged, as maybe she understands my pidgin Vietnamese.

"Okay, I will bring you something for pain." I walk away, then turn back and ask, "Can I look under the sheet?" She doesn't understand me; however, she offered no resistance when I pick up the corner of her sheet. I squelch a gasp coming up from deep inside, when a Girl Scout ditty flits through my head:

Same song, second verse, a little bit louder and a little bit worse

She needs a doctor now! I may as well be alone on the ward, as none of the Vietnamese patients speaks or understands english. I force down bitter bile rising in the back of my throat and say in my best bravado voice, "I will be right back."

I dash over to the GI ward to find Pvt. Shann and ask him, "Please find Dr. Johnson. I don't know which hooch is his, just do not come back without him!"

He salutes me, as if military formality offers an air of seriousness to the moment. I am not thinking military protocol, and I do not return the salute. "Just go!" I bark, and mutter a prayer that, considering the lateness of the hour, the good doctor is sober. Dr. Johnson may be the only GYN physician in Vietnam. And we are proud that he is assigned to the 91st.

I complain loudly, that "I am practicing medieval nursing." When I carry another basin of water to her bedside. After a second cleanup, I motion to her and she follows me to the supply room at the end of the ward. She must have walked; as I have no memory of her going from her bed to the supply closet. The room is small with enough space for a stainless-steel glass cabinet and a gurney. My charade skills prevail, and she climbs onto the gurney.

Dr. Johnson walks into the room, looks at me and asks, "Okay Judy, what's going on? "

One look at Dr. Johnson and I let out an audible sigh of relief. My report is short and to the point, "she has a profuse vaginal bleed."

Dr. Johnson looks at my patient and talks to her in a slow monotone voice. Then he tells her, "I am going to pull back the sheet, so I can get a closer look."

His hand reaches out to touch her sheet, when all-hell-brakes-loose! Her arms and legs are everywhere; with a strength that belies her tiny frame, she kicks me, square-in my chest, and I go into the glass door of the supply closet.

I lost it! The girl in 'bed seventeen's' worst nightmare now looms over her face. Me! I am like a mad dog! When I hear a litany of unlady like expletives spill out of my mouth. *Oh! Bite my tongue, you are her nurse, shut-up already.* I scream in her face, "You ingrate Gook!"

Dr. Johnson (apparently inhaled 'happy-gas') is doubled over trying to squelch a belly laugh. I glare at him and say, "At least one of us in this room is having a good time. Dr. Johnson, Sir. Will-you-get-a-grip."

He looks at me and says the obvious, "Let's get her in Post-Op, so I can find out what's going on."

I run to the GI ward, locate Pvt. Shann, and ask him to contact the NCOIC, as I am taking a Vietnamese patient to Pos-Op.

Out the door we roll; Dr. Johnson pushes, and I guide an aberrant, cranky, metal gurney, across wooden planks that cover the sand. We roll into Post-Op and are greeted by a Corpsman,

"Hey! Wha'cha-got-here?"

"Dr. Johnson needs to examine my patient. Be advised, her right foot has a mean kick."

"This tiny girl?"

My patient, subdued with the strong arms of a man on each

side, allows Dr. Johnson to do a quick pelvic. I am holding her head, *just hoping she doesn't bite me.*

"You are right Judy," the doctor states, "she is lacerated. Come see."

I look over Dr. Johnson's shoulder to view a bleeding zigzag tear the length of her vagina. He instructs the corpsmen, "She needs surgery, so get anesthesia awake and make it happen."

Guilt hangs like a cloud over me. If only I could speak her language. Would she have shared that she wants to end a pregnancy? I am humbled. As I should've comprehended the wild look in her eyes. I move to her head and apologize to her in a gentle tone, speaking a language she does not understand. She lets me hold her. While I sing her a lullaby,

"Hush now and don't say a word, Papa's gonna' by you a mockingbird."

20

Whistle Dixie

Today, I earned my pay. It's been a busy 12-hour shift, caring for two wards of patients. One ward holds the Vietnamese Army casualties and the other ward holds sixty beds filled with GI combat casualties. Early this morning, we had an influx of Infantry of the 173rd and from the 101st. After the platoon of *Sky Soldiers* and men, of the *Screamin' Eagles* learn that 'everyone' in their respective platoons survived, they relax and unwind with a bit of feisty banter, generic among Paratroopers. I smile inside; glad their spunk survived the firefights, as with the wounds some of them received, they will need a large 'hunk-of-spunk' to recover. I left the wards late tonight, but the wards lingered, like a blanket over me. I looked up and with a prayer said:

"God, I need to get away and forget everything, if only for a few minutes." I consider my options; it is too late to hang out with 'fly guy' friends at the Air Base. Besides, Rock is gone, and I need space to recover from him… or from us. I pull off my boots, smudged with the grime of today, and the endlessness of tomorrow. And slip on my flip-flops and head toward the guard tower. Our nurse hooches are situated just a stone throw from the beach. *I muse; I have always wanted a place on the beach, what sixties gal wouldn't? Perhaps a walk on the beach, relaxing with the rhythm of the waves, will drain tension off my shoulders.*

A dark, moonless night accentuates the depression that wants to own me. A distant floodlight throws long shadows over thick rolls of concertina wire to create molds of eerie netherworld forms on the sand. In the dark, I can barely make out the frame of the guard tower that overlooks the fishing village next to our perimeter.

A thought crosses my mind, "*It would ruin my day if the guard shot me!*" So, with clear diction I holler to the Corpsman who mans the tower. "Soldier, I'm a friendly. Can you see me?"

"I see you real clear, Ma-am. Watchawont? This area is off limits at night. Oh, it's you Lt. Not to worry. Are you bringing us pop-corn and sodas? Or, are you here to trim my hair?" he replied with a tease.

"Sorry, I'm not bearing gifts," I replied. Chiding myself, why didn't I bring them popcorn? Over the past months, I've brought them snacks as they stand guard. They are the lowest rank and assigned to do the uncomfortable jobs. In true military fashion, the 91st enlisted man is crossed-trained; he serves as corpsman on the wards for twelve hours, then rotates and stands perimeter guard duty at night. Not fair. One of the five guys, chosen by the Sgt. is the *"supernumerary-of-the-guard"* and gets to sleep all night. No booze for this person. Qualifying for the 'supernumerary' position depends on the favor of the Sgt. Now this is when a nurse morphs into a 'Mom' for our teen soldiers. Just before the critical inspection, the medic drops by the ward for the 'nurses' inspection. I do my best to help them look good for the 'real-deal.' I pass my hand over the face of a grinning soldier, trying to detect stubble on shaved soft peach fuzz.

"Adjust your collar so I can get a closer look at your hair."

I ceremoniously pull out my bandage scissors and become a fearsome barber as, I snip stray hair escaping down the back of the soldier's neck. Lastly, I quiz my medic on current events,

"Tell me what's happening back in 'the World." I know the Pvt. will endure relentless quizzing from the Sgt, a man known to be a grim taskmaster. The selection of the 'supernumerary of-the-guard' is the 'Army' method to instill a bit of military bearing on our young soldiers.

"No, I didn't come to hang out," I reply. "I just need permission to walk on the beach."

"Yes, Ma'am, it's okay by me. The other guard is sleeping over there on the sand. We're gonna trade places in a bit. I'll let him know that you're walking on the beach."

"Thanks Pvt. my soul appreciates you."

Pvt. Keeton, not yet twenty, didn't understand; he just handed my life back to me! Truth? Vietnam has aged me and left the corpsmen to grow in the dust of their youth. They are but eighteen-nineteen years old; draft the high school graduate, make him a soldier, teach the soldier to march, fire a rifle, then send him to Vietnam.

With permission granted, I walk a bit to get away from the

glare of floodlights, and the noise from the O' Club, where a Filipino show sings a poor rendition of the lines to Jim Croce's song:

He's bad, bad Leroy Brown...Baddest man in the whole damn town Badder than Ole' King Kong...Meaner than a junk-yard dog,

I slip off my flip-flops and listen to the waves to try and pick up their cadence; something my Dad, a WWII Merchant Marine taught me. I close my eyes and pretend I am on the other side of the world. I can almost visualize walking on a beach in the warm Gulf waters near Corpus Christi where Dad lives. I walk and walk, trying to distance myself from today, yesterday and tomorrow. I picture the water pounding on this war-torn Asian shore is part of the same great ocean that connects continents. The waves wash over the shores of lovely Carmel in California and to peace. Where men and women and children and old men and old women are not destroyed with the toss of a grenade or burnt to a crisp in the wake of a burst of napalm dropped out of a clear sky.

A junk-yard dog fares better than humanity in this ragged edge of the world.

Remember when your cares amounted to nothing? And the B's you studied for in college chemistry? And for what? The obvious answer; to swallow a salt tablet for a head-ache, and to take an anti-malaria pill every Monday. Exhaustion slips into my bones; I need to get back to my hooch. I turn around and walk back to my flip-flops. By now the guards have switched places, and my friend is asleep on the beach. However, unknown to me, my friend failed to tell the next guard that I am walking on the beach. In the dim-lit moonless night, I can barely make out the form of a large man, resting on the sand near my flip-flops. I walk closer and closer toward my flip-flops *when I hear it!*

The sharp crack of an M-16… My God, he's shooting at me! I plaster myself on the wet sand and slither into the waves crashing against the shore as the cold water of the South China Sea washes over me. Spitting sand from my mouth, I scream, "Stop! I'm American!"

In the dark I can barely see the outline of a man, holding a rifle. He breaks the fragile silence when he slowly said, "Next time, will-you-just-whistle-Dixie!"

21

Just Three Pounds

Dedicated to the platoon of the 101st 'Screamin' Eagles" RVN 68, You were recovering from malaria and were our patients in the 91st Evac. Hospital for a month. I worked the night shift. One of our pediatric patients was a small baby. You guys carried on with her as though she were your firstborn. I wrote this poem for you.

She weighed in at three pounds,
Born too early in a world so harsh.
Thrust into a land ravaged by years of war.
Love was the key that opened the door
To the heart of the proud, the 'Screamin' Eagle'
Your tough façade dissolved with her tiny smile
Your hands were so big and hers were so small
You would fuss who would take the night watch
The one to hold her and listen for her tiny baby call

I watched you, American son sent to war,
You were a lean-mean-fighting-machine
That carried the weight of the world on your young shoulders
I caught a glimpse of your soul and an oversized heart
That melted at 'just three pounds'

Thanks, gentlemen—for the memory.

22

Flak Jacket

The Mekong is an ancient river, that begins in China and powers it way south through four countries. It ends in South Vietnam and moves out to the South China Sea. Small indefatigable Vietnamese sampans, challenge U.S. Navy Swift boats to jockey for passage, on the waterways of the mighty river. Ten-foot-tall elephant grass shields the Army Evac. Hospital from the Mekong. I am working for a month, at the 29th Army Hospital, the last bastion of medical care in Vietnam.

At night, a drop light hanging over the nurses desk creates gangly shadows that want to mess with my mind. I give credence to an ominous premonition as the lyrics to a song loop through my head:

Hope you got your things together
Hope you are quite prepared to die
Looks like we're in for nasty weather
One eye is taken for an eye

I do not even like the song. Even so, the band plays on.

> *Don't go around tonight*
> *Well, it's bound to take your life*
> *There's a bad moon on the rise*

I don my cumbersome flak vest and brief my corpsman: "Should we have 'incoming' tonight, most of our patients can get under their bed and pull a blanket over them." I shudder as the word 'incoming' slid easy off my tongue. "Place their IV bottles alongside of the men that can't be moved and throw a blanket or even two blankets over them. The patients in beds four to eight, can get on the floor and pull their mattress over them. Do we have extra blankets," I slow down to ask.

The corpsman shakes his head no, then interrupted me to say, "I hope you can do this all by yourself Ma'am cause I will be over behind the refrigerator." I look hard at him, and no, he-is-not-joking.

"Just go to supply and bring back blankets." *Coward! Should be engraved on his dogtags!*

Wounded men of the 9th Infantry were admitted to our ward…one right after another. The sound of artillery shattered the silence, while tracer-bullets lit the sky, like lighting in a fierce thunderstorm. In response to the influx of admissions, I asked myself, *"how can mankind do this to each other?"* I am taken back by how quietly, each man lays, in their blood splattered, torn fatigues while patiently waiting for staff attention.

My Corpsman lied; he worked like he had nerves of steel. But he couldn't hide his raw fear, when his face and arms broke out in large red blotches.

I envy the operating-room nurses as they inspect the soldiers wounds, while ward nurses and corpsmen focus on the face of each patient and get a glimpse of the fear in their eyes.

I walk around each man's bed and encouraged them saying, "You are safe soldier. You are in an Army Hospital. Close your eyes and take a deep breath. The corpsman and I are standing guard." The encouragement offers a few men the 'okay' to pull off their heavy mask of courage and drift into a fitful sleep.

The '9th Infantry' firefight happened early in the night and the adrenalin that raced through my veins has long dissipated. I feel drained, and I must look the part, when the Nurse Officer in Charge made her rounds, she asked, "You look tired Lt. Did you have enough rest before duty?"

"Yes Ma'am, no Ma'am. I mean, I'm okay, it's just the time of the shift when the ward is quiet."

"I'll man the desk so you can relax for a few minutes, why don't you rest on the empty bed over there?" she said and pointed to an unoccupied bed.

She made me an offer I did not refuse, as exhaustion wants to own me. I lay down on the bare mattress, next to a patient attached to the mask and hose of a 'Bird-Respirator.' I quickly doze off to the regular rhythm of the respirator, triggered by the patient's cyclic breathing. He must have held his breath, when the cadence of air-flow changed.

I bolt upright, and in a daze, I holler, "*God, is he going to breathe?!*"

Fatigue didn't rule. I thanked the NOIC for spotting me. She's gone a mere ten minutes, when the long blades of a Cobra gunship roared overhead. The helicopter continues the search for the perpetrator of tonight's firefight. For a brief moment I am fascinated with the tracers and the puffs that stream poetry in the sky. My Corpsman and I orientate our patients to reality, while the blades of the helicopter tries to distort their dreams and tug at their 'twilight' thoughts.

I morph into a barking 'Drill Sgt' when my corpsman and I wake the patients, with a scream, *"Get-under-your-bed-on-the-floor-now!"*

Warrior instinct drives most of the ambulatory patients to the floor. My mind checks off a litany of tasks. *Place intravenous bottles by the side of patients tethered to their beds and drape them with wool Army blankets.*

A sudden glare of lights from the Cobra, splits the darkness, and pressure from the long blades of the helicopter flattens the elephant grass. The Cobra, needing precise aim, gets help from the Air Force. In a short space of time, the historic, Berlin-Airlift, war-horse 'the C-47, 'Puff the Magic Dragon' flies over-head. The C-47 makes a steep left bank and the "Dragon's" Gatlin guns rain down deadly streams of fire on the target.

The battle is over, and *Victor Charlie was exposed. Hell exacts a wage. My spirit 'in the presence of death was overcome with* 'the holy' when a moment of eerie silence filled the air, as the souls of Victor Charlie reach out to meet their maker. I lift my face upward and am surprised when my soul spills out a prayer:

"God, You are truth and the life. Have mercy on their souls. Away with a dogma," I pray, "that wants to sully the sacred moment when their souls turn to meet You!"

When the 'all-clear' sounds, our battle-weary patients, stand up and flop back to their beds. The hospital did not suffer a direct hit, even so, in the cool night air, my fatigues were drenched with sweat. It is 0600! We survived another night in Vietnam. I flipped the ward lights on and waken our patients to another day in Vietnam. The Armed Forces Radio spins a recording and Neil Diamond sings:

> *I thank the Lord for the nighttime*
> *to forget the day… A day of uptight time*
> *Baby, chase it away…I get relaxation*
> *It's a time to groove… I thank the Lord*
> *for the nighttime…I thank the Lord for you*

23

Then There is Red

I don't remember your name. I called you Red, as you had a crop of bright red hair and blue-blue eyes. Your folks raised their freckled-face son, to be strong. Your beliefs were shaken when you served in the 9th Infantry. Your prayer was simple,

"God help me to live to see another day."

You went on to explain that, "to talk to the officer-in-charge about my fear, would be a sure ticket to LBJ at Saigon (Long Binh Jail).

Nights, when you couldn't sleep, you sat by the nurse's desk and words slid like a river right off your tongue. You introduced me to your family, and to the faith they instilled in you. After high school you reported to the selective service because, "I didn't want the military breathing down my neck, so I reported to the draft board. But I never thought that I could be this fearful. Every evening, when the sun goes down, I have to make myself suck-it-up till sunrise. Days are not hard; just know that night follows day, and there it is again. Dark."

I cringe when you describe the challenges that face you, "I can tolerate the tablets that changes the taste of water, and the insect stings and the bites from, God-knows-what from the crawling, flying creatures. But Lt. I am most afraid when I have to live another night."

To help me appreciate your anxiety, your words paint a picture. "Close your eyes Lt. Now, see yourself sitting on the yellow line that divides a two-way road. It's night; and cars are coming and going past you at break-neck-speed. You are dressed in black and concealed by the lights of most of the cars. Do you sweat? Does bitter bile burn your throat?"

In the early morning, after my shift, we went into the empty chapel, where I played the old tunes of the church on the small electric piano. We sang one hymn after another.

"Just as I Am…He Leadeth Me…Blessed Assurance…I Need Thee Every Hour."

And then from somewhere deep inside, you cried, and I cried with you. You went back to your platoon with the 9th Infantry. I will never know if raising your cries to God brought peace to your soul. I prayed for you, Red, and I prayed for myself as well.

24

"Rock"

We met in a room crowed with rowdy men in crumpled flight suits. A nod of the head would have done for our first introduction into each other's lives. However, Rock, you went one step beyond; in a world where propriety and manners had taken a backseat, you reached out to grip my hand, and said, "hello."

I recalled an introduction to the fighter plane as I shared with you that I was on duty the night when you and your wingman flew the F-100 the over 91st Hospital. "It was late; time for the geckos to come out and play a tune, when you and your wingman made a special flight and 'lit the burner' over our hospital. The noise split the sky and men sleeping in the enlisted quarters bolted from the barracks in all shades of dress to flattened themselves on the sand. I thought, "must have been Rock and his wingman just saying hello." Of course, I lied through my teeth when I denied even knowing any air-force types.

"Oh, yes!" you confessed. "That low flyby over the hospital was crazy to pull off, as we could have collided with Dust-Off helicopters."

You quickly changed the topic and went on to say, "Vietnam is a beautiful country, especially when you get close to Laos. Before a mission, my focus is on the ordnance we would be carrying and whether we would draw a good target."

You continued, saying, "Helping the troops when they were in danger brought a thrill… It may sound trite, but it's accurate to say, I am young, a college grad and trusted to fly the 'Hun.' What an adventure! The trick to night flying was the more I did it, the more comfortable I am. It's harder to go fast and hit a target when visibility is zilch. The night missions made me think harder about not screwing up. To varying degrees, we all shook off the close calls. If you dwelt on them, they could impair your performance and your mental well-being. The risk of the mission just went with the privilege of flying."

"Tell me about the night-creature calls?" I interrupted and asked.

"Fosnot and I started the 'creature' calls. It all came about when we took a couple of jets to Tainan, on the island of Taiwan, for periodic maintenance. They told us there were no jets for us to fly back in-country, so, we decided to go to Taipei for a little R&R. We checked into the Golden Palace Hotel and called Tainan each morning to see if they had any jets for us. After four or five days (the number is hazy), they told us that our squadron was pissed and there would be a C-130 going to Tuy Hoa the next day."

You go on to say, "as expected, when we got back to Tuy Hoa, we pulled night alert. Normally, night alert was a one-to three-night ordeal, then we would go back to flying day missions. We gave ourselves the Bat and Owl call signs the morning when we came into the squadron from flying multiple night alerts. Our names weren't on the schedule for night alert, but the Bat and the Owl were written on the board. That led to the 'Lieutenants Protection Club.' There were about six lieutenants that adopted a 'night-creature' call name. Possum, Gecko, and… can't name them off hand. Our good nature was a bard song in the making."

He went on with his story. "Fosnot had emotional problems. Do you remember the night when he listened to his demons and drove the squad scooter in the open door of his trailer, through the bathroom and out the other door of the trailer? This amazing feat was done with the same finesse when he flew the Hun."

I admitted to you, Rock, that, "You were my first love. I will always remember your hands. You shared that they, "white-knuckled the stick to drop a deadly load on the target, then barrel-rolled to miss deadly flak, aimed to bring you down."

It was your hands that "stilled my anxious heart as they massaged away the anxiety of living and loving in war." No one knew how much you meant to me, Rock, not even you, as I held my cards close to my chest.

You 'DEROSed' back to the 'World" and our good times faded into a special memory as I 'white-knuckled my grip' and continued caring for the men wounded in combat.

25

TACOS

In January 1968, as a result of the Pueblo Crisis, the 188th Tactical Fighter Squadron and approximately 250 maintenance and support personnel were deployed to Tuy Hoa Air Base Vietnam. The 188th flew over 6000 combat sorties in the F-100C Super Sabre. They amassed over 630 medals and decorations before release from federal active duty in June 1969.[1]

The Tacos made the men of the New Mexico Air National Guard proud. I enjoyed their jocular manners as laughter really is the best medicine. Major Walt Jarret's 'Hun' caught the tops of trees on a flight back to Tuy Hoa. Recall that the 31st Air-Wing was dead-set to discipline the rowdy 188th pilots. Walt related the meat of their conversation.

I asked him, "Were you upset when Col. Aust called you on the 'tree' protocol?"

---

[1] Wikipedia

He replied, "Naw! I just looked at him and asked, "*Well! Whatchegonnado? Make me a Major and send me to Vee Et Nam?*"

I teased Walt about his Texas accent saying that, "Walt, I'm a Texan and I can talk, *jes like you but my accent is different, 'cause I can turn the west Texas drawl off and you can't.*"

They pull out their guitars to serenade me with:

*"You're an Angel Judy, you're a darling.
You're the sweetest flower that grows.
You came down from heaven just to make us happy here.
You pushed away our troubles and you smiled away our tears.
It seems that we've always known you, tho' we've never met before.
So, you'll be in our hearts little dear to stay forever more!"*

Of course, these men were my among my favorite Squadrons. About the 'lost refrigerator, when '31st Wing' tried without success, to locate the missing refrigerator. I remember the day they stole it and I'm still amazed at their savvy. My take goes like this, the Tacos eyed a refrigerator, in a holding area, and commandeered an Airman to load it up and have it delivered to their communal party room. Just that simple.

Friendship with the men at the 188th and the 309th grew into a memory with a large bow on top.

Captain Michael Adams was killed in action and Major Bobby Neeld and First Lieutenant Mitchell Lane are listed as missing in action

Michael and I were friends; valuable when living in a combat zone. The 188th had a memorial in the base chapel for Michael. No one scolded me when tears spilled down my face. I cried for the loss of a special friend and I cried for the men of the 188th Squadron that respected combat-protocol, "No-Crying-in-Vietnam." They held their tears and cried later…at a wake of sorts, over a beer or two.

26

SAPPER Attack

I donned my 'duty-mask' that smiled when caring for our soldier patients. I am mindful to abide by an unwritten dogma, *"There is no crying in Vietnam!"* I am the lowly 2nd Lieutenant, in charge of two wards, the GI and the Vietnamese. I give the Vietnamese patients a hello and a nod to their smiles that reveal brown stained teeth, caused by a lifetime of chewing opium beetle-nut

Beds on the GI ward are filled with row after row of soldiers; many are teenagers, just out of high school. I wear a mask that smiles when caring for them; I have trained my smile to squelch tears that try to stream down my face. Our patients wear light blue-army pajamas and a non-issued mask of courage. These teen men share a bond with all casualties of war. The cocky, nonchalant mask they wear is vital to them as the dogtags that dangle around their necks. 'Don't mean nothin' is an understood idiom in this war-ravaged country.

Most of the patients are fresh out of high school. Life on the GI ward changes as day morphs into night. The light from a single bulb, hangs over the nurse desk, and creates shadows on the ward at night. Daytime hours have no shadows. It's the shadows of night that messes with their minds when sleep owns the unconscious fears of the soldier. When asleep they relive the terror of the dark night, when *no-one-lit-a-smoke*. I stay wide of the soldiers' arms and legs as they box the air over their head while reliving the battle that almost cost their life. And I shudder with the screams that holds their sleeping thoughts in a vice-grip.

I welcome being off-duty. So, this is how life happens; when I work six shifts of twelve-hour duty, I get thirty-six hours off. No early wake up! I walked the dirt road between Phu Hiep Compound and Tuy Hoa Air Base and snag a ride to the 309th Squadron.

The two mile stretch of dirt road, from Phu Hiep Compound, to Tuy Hoa Air Base, borders the village of Phu Hiep, with well laid concertina-wire fence. I muse that, *"The wire fence seems utterly inadequate. Will rolls of concertina wire protect us from Phu Hiep village?"*

By the time I arrive at the base, my mask has changed. I am now wearing my 'friendly' relaxed mask.

A pilot, just back from a mission, greets me, "Hi Judy, how did your shift go last night? You're pulling night duty, aren't you?"

"Thanks for asking," I respond with a cheerful mask, that knows how to lie. "The night went well, and I'm feeling good."

The men of the 309th treat me with care, as do the guys in the 188th New Mexico Air Guard, their sister squadron. Friendship with the guys began when we nurses responded to an invite of 91st nurses to a 309th Squadron Steak Night. Enjoying the company of Air Force guys was even better than dining on a charcoal steak, as I did not realize my miss for Air Force people, men, wearing crumpled flight suits.

Tonight I'm billeted in Lt. Col Whitford's room while he is in the Philippines. Col. Renshaw shares the other side of the trailer. He woke me to say, "Judy there is a Red Alert siren. You can stay here, and I will come get you if needed. Is this okay with you?"

"It's okay with me Sir," I reply, "Is there by any chance another blanket?" He brought me a blanket and I quickly went back to sleep.

A sapper attack from the Viet Cong, on Tuy Hoa Air Base was rare, however, it happened. The V.C. dug under the concertina wire that surrounded the base and quickly destroyed several planes parked in the revetments. They did not make it back to Phu Hiep village; as the Air Force MP, riddled them with lead and plastered their bodies on the concertina wire that separated Phu Hiep village from Tuy Hoa Air Base.

This happened while I slept like a baby, in an air-conditioned trailer, and I didn't even dream.

27

Wingman

I met "Moose," a good-humored guy, at the 309th Dustys Pub after my shift at the 91st. He shared that Jerry's wingman did not make it back from their flight. When tears spilled down my face, he looked straight at me to say, "You can't cry, Judy. Remember: *There is no crying in Vietnam!*"

In my heart of hearts, I felt like this might happen to the 309th, the squadron of men I had grown to love.

"Where's Jerry now?" I asked.

"He's somewhere out on the beach. Tom (a 309th pilot), was with him till Jerry told him to leave," Moose replied. "We called you, as you are not a pilot, you're not Air Force, and he is close to you, so maybe he'll let you hang around."

Of all the friends I'd made with the 309th Jerry was the one who'd been transparent with me. A friend is a precious commodity in life. I called him a friend.

I opened a bottle of beer, grabbed it by the neck and crossed the asphalt road that ran parallel to the surf of the South China Sea. You were alone with your knees pulled up to your chest. I handed you the beer—not that you haven't already put away more than a few—you can use just one more. You took a swig of the beer, then rambled, talking to yourself as much as to me.

"Bottom-line, I called the strike, and because of me, he is dead. I've 268 missions, and I should know better. Right? He's new in-country; even so, we had the makings for a good team. You can't teach passion; it's fire in your belly. Maybe it's me, I am all fired up when leading a mission. I'm one of the best leads in the squadron. So, there's no peaceful reason I should do this, 'cept I'm a gung-ho fighter jock; an immature college grad that flies a five-million-dollar combat jet. Face it: I'm an arrogant mother, a prisoner to my pride. There is nothing that will bring Vince back."

"Slow down, Jerry. Breathe," I said as I step back a bit from his angry outburst.

"Slow down. Breathe! Vince can't breathe. He is dead! And it's my fault. If only I had not told him to go in for another pass. Like the know-it-all-son-of-a-bitch that I am, I gave him the okay. It is just hard to grasp. You will never understand how fucking bad I feel. I gave him the command. I told him it was okay to make another pass; gave him the green light to roll in and learn as you go! Flak was everywhere, and regs dictate that we can leave the scene. Shit! There were no troops in danger, just a thin line of fucking NVA trucks carrying ammo. We were not even supporting grunts! Were troops in danger, then maybe it would have been different. Bottom line, I called the strike, and because of me Vince-is-dead!"

I know your anger needs to come out, and who better to rant against than an Army type? Then your voice dropped to a whisper, as pain ripped through your soul. Something cautioned me to stay close as you *welcome death when you hurt the most. You talked in low tones, almost a whisper, as if when you talked too loud, the words would be grabbed in the air and not be real.*

"I'm a gung-ho fighter pilot, poised to receive a Silver Star, commending me for the 268 missions I've flown in Vietnam. I swear, I will never take the damn medal out of its case. If Vince can't walk around with medals on his chest, then I won't either!"

With your knees pulled tight to your chest I gave your shoulder a squeeze and walked away.

God can do wonders with a broken heart, when He has all the pieces. I will cry with you, Jerry, until our tears run dry.

28

R and R

Carol, my Oklahoma Army nurse friend, was due to rotate back home soon. We were miles apart as, Carol served at the far north end of Vietnam, while I served for a month in the 29th Evac Hospital, way south of Saigon. So, the trusty Army phone, 'the landline' enabled us to put the finishing touches on our upcoming R&R in Japan. Or so we thought.

Our week away from Vietnam got off on the wrong foot as Carol hit the Tachikawa Base Exchange in Japan in search of a bra. There were none her size. Nada. Carol lamented loudly while in the base beauty shop, "Like a new nurse in-country, I hung my 'other' bra on the clothesline, outside our quarters." Carol failed to mention the clothesline was at the 18th Surgical Hospital, just fourteen miles from the DMZ. The story goes on: "My only 'other' bra was stolen off the clothesline. I just knew that the base exchange would have a bra my size (big). The clerk told me they had sold two large bras just that day."

Back at the hotel, Carol answered a knock on the door, where she greeted a Caucasian woman. Carol's jaw dropped in wonder as the woman thrust a package into Carol's hands, saying, "I bought these bras from the exchange yesterday, and I believe they belong to you." The woman wouldn't allow my friend to pay for them.

With the bra shortage taken care of, we were off to a grand week, except Tokyo was snowed in. It was winter in Japan, and winter where we were from in Oklahoma pales in comparison to the harsh Japanese winter. Even the fast bullet train was shut down. Not to waste a day of R&R, I convinced Carol to fly to Sapporo, a large city on the island of Hokkaido. The mountains around Sapporo boast of superb skiing.

We checked into a fine hotel and shopped at a Japanese-style flea market, where we bought a couple of sweaters and ski jackets. Come morning, we woke early and took a taxi to the closest ski slopes. Carol had never been on skis, and there need be another chapter to detail the only time I skied. On the way to our adventure, I admired huge ice sculptures, about thirty feet tall, at several places around the city.

Way different from the heat of Vietnam, I mused.

So, this is how two gals from the flatlands of Oklahoma set out to enjoy the day on the ski slopes. However, as we tried and we tried just to stand up, the world literally slid out from under our skis. The shy Japanese skiers tried to conceal their laughter.

Then it happened. I was not hallucinating. Near us were three men talking in English. Not one to be shy, I asked, "Are you

English?" And, without taking another breath, I added, "Can we join you?"

The person doing the most talking was a ski instructor, and the other two men were his students. He said, "Ladies, you are welcome to join us, please."

The men were from the Mideast. The ski lessons were at an end when the gracious Iranian men invited Carol and me to dinner that evening. We gave them a hotel card, penned in Japanese, and went back to our room. We waited and we waited for our dates to come to the door. Then the phone rang. I answered and a voice said, "Judy, are you coming?"

Duh. Carol and I had waited in our room while our dates for the evening were in the lobby. I hoped this misunderstanding would be the only difference between two American Army nurses and two Mideastern Sheiks from Iran. We met the men in the lobby, hailed a taxi and set off to a memorable evening. We enjoyed dinner at a Japanese restaurant. You know, the place where one sits on the floor to eat from a very low table. The Mideastern gentlemen were at ease. Me? I was on my knees and kept shifting side-to-side, just trying to get comfortable.

The restaurant was a dinner-dance place. I enjoy dancing; however, the difference between our cultures stifled the evening and I told my date that I didn't care to dance. I was not acquainted with the people of the East, still a gripping story of the customs of Middle-Eastern men went through my mind. I did not dare mention to Carol the fear that loomed in my head; had we been the least bit inclined, the two men would have made us their American brides.

I politely pushed the Iranian men away with skills honed while living in a country of men. The hour was late and realizing that we two ladies were not interested in a life-long relationship, the men called us a taxi. I was ever so glad that they lacked a "wife network" here in Sapporo. *Or, perhaps,* I shudder to think, *the men from Iran had a harem of women in Japan, and Carol and I simply slipped their grasp.*

29

HERCULES

The nurse working the day shift relieved me early this morning so I could join the crew of the C-130 Air Force plane on the flight line at Tuy Hoa AB. The mission of the C-130 was to on-load an Air Force Flight Nurse team and transport combat-wounded soldiers from Army MASH Hospitals to the 95th Evacuation Hospital. At DaNang the C-130 gained an Aeromed Crew. The Aeromed crew was in charge of the fuselage the entire day. With cursory introductions done, I approached the Captain to ask, "I realize my fatigues are a dead giveaway. I'm an Army nurse that once-upon-a-time was an Air Force flight nurse, and I request permission to work with your medical team."

We exchanged hellos and he said, "With your worn fatigues, I'm sure you have cared for your share of combat casualties. Of course, you will be a helping hand to augment our skeletal medical crew. Here, you can be the nurse for six litters and several canvas sling-seats along the fuselage. This means that both ambulatory and litter-bound soldiers will be in your care. If you have questions, just ask and one of us will find the answer." He then flashed a grin to say, "just do as we do, and you'll be all right."

I am puzzled with his last statement, 'just do as we do and you'll be alright' But then I am so naïve, so I shrug it off.

The entire day, our C-130 did puddle-jumps all over I Corps. The plane didn't reach the cooler air of a higher elevation. However, this C-130 boasted a 'manhole cover' on the ceiling of the flight-deck.

The loadmaster said that, "the air-crew flies with the cover open in an attempt to infuse cooler air back to the 'lions-den' of the fuselage where the Aeromed crew was working." How hot was it? It was so hot that everyone in the medical team, the Capt. included, worked with their fatigue shirts off.

I smiled at the captain's grin and his dry humor.

"Oh! And Lieutenant, just do as we do, and you'll be okay."

The voice of our Aircraft Commander came clear over the mike. "We are approaching the 18th Surgical Hospital. This will be a quick turnaround. The patients on the tarmac will be loaded immediately. In Charlie's wet dreams, he is waiting for us. We will not wait for the bastard, as the first round he lobs will miss our plane, and the second round he lobs will hit us dead-center. However, we will not give the son-of-a-bitch the pleasure of bringing this plane down. Load those on the tarmac and the ramp doors close and we-are-airborne. Charlie will have to be quick. If he so much as scratches his butt, we are but a speck in the sky."

The message from the AC emphasizes the danger of the 18th Surgical Hospital, a mere fourteen miles from the DMZ. I accept a litter patient, an NVA (North Vietnamese Army) soldier. I swallowed hard, as I was out of my comfort zone, when my eyes met those of the enemy. The fact that he is wounded offers no consolation. I clearly understood him when he spoke in Vietnamese, "Twi Wie, Nook! Nook."

The wounded soldier asked for water. In my mind ran a line I learned in Sunday School: *'If your enemy is thirsty, give him water.'*

"Give him water?"

"He is thirsty Judy. He asked for water. He didn't ask for a weapon." Maybe kindness is a weapon, I reasoned. I carried a small Dixie cup of water to him when a Marine, strapped in a sling-seat, leaned over and with a dry raspy-dry voice said, *"One sip of water! You give that fuckin' son-of-a-bitch one sip of water, and he's dead!"*

30

A Marine Firebase Camp

Spending a day with the Air Force Flight Nurses and corpsmen help me understand the rational that precluded women from flying in-country air evacuation. It was not lost on me, that the medical team did-double-duty transporting litters, heavy with the weight of a wounded soldier.

After parting with the Air Force medical squad at DaNang, the Tuy Hoa crew morphed into a mail-carrier; as they delivered sacks of mail to the troops at a Marine Firebase Camp, a place that provides the Marine a place to shower, sleep and eat mess-hall food. We delivered the mail-sacks when the engine of our 'Hercules' C-130 roared, ready for take-off. The engines stalled, when the voice of our AC comes over the mike, "Lt. would you mind just stepping off the plane and give these guys a look at an American female, to help them remember what they are fighting for?"

In response to the request of our AC, I climbed down the steps, below the flight deck, and stood on the muddy PCP. I was surprised; it's as though the men had never seen a round-eyed woman, as every window in the two-story building was packed with faces of Marines. Then a man wearing Marine field fatigues and a flat-top ball hat (indigenous to the Navy and Marines) walked toward me. I watched him fall into a muddy ditch, climb out of the ditch, not taking his eyes off me, in his mud-covered fatigues, kept walking toward me. A voice inside me said, "You are the Soldiers' mom, wife, sister and girlfriend wrapped up in one." To honor them, I turned to face the men in the windows and gave them a slow salute. The Marine who had fallen into the ditch lifted a muddy hand and returned my salute.

31

When a Lady Has To Pee

Our final mission of the day was to deliver mail to an Army Outpost. We landed on the PCP close to a thin American flag. That showed both the direction and the velocity of the wind. Today, 'Ole' Glory' hung limp. In a jeep, on the way to deliver the mail sacks I viewed, a 'field-piss-pot'; a waist-high cement 'V' shaped barrier, strategically positioned where two roads intersect. I am amazed with the convenience of war; when a soldier, weighted with a heavy bandolier of arsenal, could stand and take a leak. We were introduced to the C.O. a Cpt. One of the Air Force persons told the Army Cpt. that "the lady with them (me) needs to use the restroom."

"No problem," says the Cpt. when he turned to a Pvt. close by to say, "Pvt. show the Lieutenant where she can use the restroom."

The Pvts' face drained from pink to pale when he asked, "Sir? The Vietnamese outhouse?"

"Yes," the Cpt. replied, "does the order confuse you?"

A command given is a command received, so the Pvt. and I walked to a small wooden hut located apart from the area of operation. Great. This meager base boasts of a 'ladies room.' The Pvt. pulled the door to the hut open, and quickly let it close, but not before I viewed mounds and mounds of crystallized urine.

"Well so much for the ladies room, I am not as agile as the Vietnamese women."

The Pvt. assigned to help me was creative, "Ma'am, this being a sandlot, we can hold up a blanket anywhere you want so's you can go in private." I need to pee so bad I hurt, making it hard to follow the Pvt's line of thought, until he showed me how they could make it happen. Now there were more guys, teamed up to help the Lt. pee. I quickly decide to use several blankets, as the Firebase Camp boasts of a lot of traffic and I was sure my impromptu toilet would be a show-stopper. So, four guys, held up Army wool blankets, turned their backs to me, to create a square. Tah-dah! In this Army outpost, in the middle of 'Nowhere, Vietnam' the men created for me, a private toilet. I embarrassed myself when I peed, and I peed.

After delivering the mail, the crew brought their C-130 'Hercules' back to Tuy Hoa. The loadmaster volunteered to drive me to the 91st Evac Hospital. I didn't share the day with my hooch-mates as; there are no words to help them understand, that the Army medical care we offer is but a 'cog' in the care of men wounded in combat.

32

Montagnard Smiles

My ride was in the back-seat in the "Bird Dog," a small Cessna single-engine airplane. The pilot, Smoke Greene, completes the cockpit check; when a gust of wind grabbed the plane, picked it up, twirled it around, then set it down. But not before splashing my face with topped-off fuel.

"You okay Jude? We can scrub the mission if you want."

I wipe fuel off my face and say, "I am good to go."

Friendship with Smoky led to, "Come on, fly with me and I will take you to a Special Forces Camp in the Central Highlands." Just that easy. The 91st Hospital was relocating to Chu Lai, so I was not scheduled to work for two and half days. I was pumped to make a trip to the Highlands and see how the little brown tribal people do life. It's a short flight when Smoke lands the 'Bird Dog' near a large building. He made the introductions, then told me, "Jud, I'll be back in a couple of hours. Enjoy." Then off he goes into a clear blue sky. Wait, I didn't plan to be dropped off. Oh well. Doesn't change a thing. Pinch me. I am at a Green Beret Camp.

The Special Forces camp, located, in the Central Highlands of Vietnam, is positioned between a Vietnamese and a Montagnard village. Cpt. Raymond, the Officer of the Green Berets, changes into fatigues, and we take a jeep, to the Montagnard village. He briefs me on the people,

"These tribal people are set apart from other tribes, as they speak their own language. The Vietnamese consider the Montagnard as 'second-class citizens' much like the settlers in early America, viewed the Indian population, a couple of centuries ago."

"Seems barbaric," I comment.

"They're smart, so don't judge them by their looks. They live like their ancestors lived, decades back, but they are quick studies, loyal to their families and to Americans. When the sun goes down it's good to know who you can trust."

On the road to the Montagnard village, we attract attention; when young Vietnamese guys run after our jeep, pull up their meager shirts and holler, "Thi-Wie! Thi-Wie!"

"What's this about?" I question Cpt. Raymond.

"They seem to know you. They're calling you Lieutenant and I don't know why they are pulling their shirts up."

"Oh! I get it," I exclaimed. "These Vietnamese were our patients. They are pointing to their scars. Small world."

With the Cpt. at my side I feel safe.

He parked the jeep at the end of a dirt road. We walk to the Montagnard village, when the Cpt. says, "Something's not right, as they are always here. It's your hair." He quickly surmises.

"My hair? What about my hair?"

"Your blond hair. They've never seen a person with blond hair. Maybe they're frightened," he explained, "the Montagnard's have 'voo-doo' dolls. You may be the first live 'voo-doo' they've encountered."

"A 'voo-doo' doll," I think out loud, "what an eerie thought."

We walk down the path toward the village when a girl runs out of a thatched-roof hut and hollers, "Lu-ten-ant! Hong!"

I turn to the Cpt. and give voice to the thought going through my head,

"You said you guys were not 'that' close to these people?"

"We aren't. I swear, I don't know how she knows English."

I did not have time to puzzle it out, when she grabbed my arm and pulled me inside the hut. I am taken back, when I recognize her as the girl our hospital discharged six months ago. Following the orders of our CO; we had to find a place for her. It was a sad day when we sent her away, with slim hope of connecting with her family.

Hong was excited for me to meet the woman in the small hut,

"Hong moo-der."

"Your mother?"

"Yah" she blurts out, "Hong Moo-der."

For six months after '68 Tet Offensive, Hong had no contact with her family. She didn't even know if they were alive. I left the security of my base to learn that Hong found her mother and that they live together in relative safety, then my 'gutsy' trip to the Vietnam Highlands is a treasure!

My eyes, now accustomed to the dim lit hut, note a delicate brush and mirror set on a bench. Tears tumble down my face when I realize I am looking at the 'brush and mirror' set we nurses gave Hong when she left the hospital. And there it is, still in its pristine package. With Hong at my side, the journey deep into the Montagnard village takes on a life of its own. Hong's leg-bones are 'rickets-soft,' a condition that renders her almost a cripple. No problem. We trade shoes: I wore her Jesus shoes (flip-flops made from an old tire) while Hong, slipped her dusty feet into my boots as though she were *Cinderella* and my black leather combat boots were her glass slippers.

With Hong at my side, the little brown people came out of their grass huts to greet me. Because of the wet monsoon season, the huts are built off the ground on sturdy bamboo stilts. 'Curiosity' (theirs as well as mine) pulls me to crawl inside the Montagnard hut to see where the little people 'do life.' In one corner of the hut is a large hammock with a small charcoal stove in the other corner. Everyone is topless, with rags that cover them from the waist down. Some of the younger children are naked or wore a shirt with no pants. I muse that the absence of clothes on the little ones takes care of potty training. The woman of the hut has a baby suckling her breast. The people look well; they are a bit curious, still, they smiled all over. Yes; genuine describes their smiles. I felt like I would be safe in their care. I walk my friend, Hong, back to her hut, trade shoes and tell her and the 'gentle people' a forever good-bye.

I turn to Cpt. Raymond to express my thoughts, "Thank you for taking me to the village, now it makes sense, why the tribal peoples keep to the themselves. Can I ask a favor? Maybe, Hong could walk if she had a set of crutches. If I can get her crutches, will you teach her how to use them?"

"Ask whatever you want." Cpt. Raymond says, "It's good to see the Montagnard accept you. As you are the only person they've ever seen with blond hair. You'll be in their stories for a very long time."

33

The Green Beret Medic

Smoke cannot get back to pick me up until tomorrow. No worry, as I am not on the work schedule for two days. The Cpt. offers, "I have the only private quarters, so I'll man the radio tonight, and you can stay in my room."

I feel welcomed. Life doesn't hit 'pause' when the Special Forces Medic receives a call from the Big-gun 105mm Howitzer close by, *"We have a sick baby. Come now!"*

A baby? At an Artillery Base? I climb in the jeep with the Green Beret medic. We are greeted at the gate by an armed guard. He ushers our jeep through rolls and rolls of concertina wire. I am struck by the raw loneliness and the filth of the base, seeped in dust-red dust. We are led down dirt steps to a large bunker.

A soldier, holding a baby shares, "Someone from the Vietnamese village brought this baby to us saying, no-die." He looked straight at me as he hands me a small, 'rag-doll-limp' baby, and says, "Baby no die! You bic?" (baby no die, you understand) He goes on to say, "the village medicine man treated the baby until she was almost dead." His bleak report sends shivers up my spine. And the Special Forces Medic and me, must breathe life into this baby? Then the 'big-gun' fires and clumps of dirt, from the boarded ceiling of the bunker, peppers our hair and fatigues. I pray inside my heart, 'God, don't let this baby die.' She needs a miracle" Maybe my prayer was spoken aloud, as the Medic looks at me, to share the obvious. "I wish they would have brought her here sooner. This baby needs a miracle." I bundle the tiny baby in an old Army towel, and climb out of the dim lit bunker, into a gray, grimy hot summer day. I hold her close, as though life in me will permeate into her tiny body.

Everyone at the Special Forces camp hovers over our tiny patient. She is barely breathing as dehydration demands a payment. We called "Dust-Off" and in short time our ears welcome the blades of a Huey helicopter. The baby is lifted off to the 67th Army Hospital where she will receive care by tender, skillful hands. I am filthy, and I look the part. One of the guys directs me to a back room and says,

"Our shower is back here. Take your time as you have all the privacy you need."

I slip out of my fatigues, stand under the water as mud from my hair and off my body, swirls down the drain. I step out of the shower, shake dirt off my fatigues and put them back on. As with the Fighter pilots at Tuy Hoa, the men of the Special Forces Camp have given me a gift.

Respect.

34

Green Beret Sleep Over

If daytime was fascinating, spending the night at the Camp vied for attention. For protection, all lights, except a small light by the radio, are off. As a girl in the Camp, I am offered the captains single room, while he mans the radio. The rest of the men head to their quarters carved deeper underground. The captain's room is the first one in the bunker; to make it homey, the packed dirt walls are paneled with Sears-and Roebuck's best faux wood. The experiences of the day are amazing; I am bone tired. The light from a Teac reel-to-reel tape player gives off a soft glow in the room. I doze off when something dive-bombed the bed. I grab a flashlight and 'lit-up' the largest cock-roach known to man!

"This will not do Mister Roach. This place is all yours!" Without fanfare, I pull on my fatigues, grab a sheet and go out of the bunker to sit in the glow of a full moon. I chide myself, "What's with me?" Self-talk prattles in my head. "I-am-target-practice, as here I sit, wrapped in a white sheet with the moon as bright as day." I head for the darkened Camp building and greet Cpt. Raymond, monitoring the radio. "Sorry to disturb you," I tell him, "but a huge roach drove me out of the bunker."

"I should have warned you, Judy, but they don't come around every night. They're looking for scraps of food. I was hoping they wouldn't bother you." I must have looked tired as he went on to say, "You can sleep on the porch-sofa. Let me know if you need anything."

"Thanks. I'll be okay." I tell him as I head for the porch.

The sofa, at the end of a screened-in porch, is protected by a wall of sandbags stacked four-feet high. My eyes barley close when I hear a soft, rustling sound. I aim my trusty flashlight in the direction of the noise, and stare into the beady eyes of a rat. The light startles the rat and me as well! He-is-the-size-of-a-cat! "This is just not my night. Rats." I tell the Cpt. "I should be used to them by now."

"You can try laying down, in the breeze, under the ceiling fan, maybe it's varmint free."

I am so tired, the floor looks soft. I drift off into an exhausted sleep. Come on daylight, this night has been surreal. When a man's voice crashes my dream.

"Good Morning." I hear the voice say,

I look around to orientate myself with reality. There was no man in my night; however, I heard a man's voice. My sleepy thoughts say. The 'voice' is talking to me. I wake enough, to grasp, that I am not in my hooch. I am in the Vietnam Highlands at a Special Forces Camp. In the past twenty-four hours, I have learned how life is lived on the other side of the world. I have changed; I will never be the same again.

35

The Aussie and the Bomb

The Special Forces cook is a genius. With sparse ingredients, he set before us a sumptuous omelet. I dare not ask where he got the eggs, or even if they were eggs. On leaving, the Sargent stuck a paper in my hand with a phone number scribbled on it. "Not my number," he quickly explains, "it's my Mom's. Give her a call to let her know that I'm alive and well."

Smoke lands the Bird Dog on a dirt strip near the Camp building,

"Your taxi's here, Jud' I'm on a short leash, so we gotta get."

I climb in the back seat of the small plane, while Smoke instructs me on the two-channel radio, then he goes on to say,

"I'm coordinating with an Aussie Air Force fighter jock that is training a Vietnamese Airforce pilot. I will be in radio contact with them so, be quiet and everything will be fine."

Up, up and away! Smoke, a seasoned USAF pilot, handles the

'Bird Dog' with a light touch as he flies the small plane back and forth just above the treetops, dipping deep to one side, then deep to the other side. "See that 'Papasan' sunning on the roof of the hooch?"

I didn't answer; while Smoke is enjoying the moment, I am busy keeping down the scrumptious breakfast I shared with the Special Forces. With Smoke's nimble hand and quick eye, he located a good target for the Aussie. I listened, as he makes radio contact with the fighter plane, flying somewhere above us. The Aussie instructed the Vietnamese pilot then tells Smoke to,

"mark the target and we'll do our best."

Then a Vietnamese voice comes across the headset, "Sit-eem up hot, arm, nose teel, I got you, een-site."

Smoke radios back, "You're looking good. Cleared in hot, come-on-down-and-pickle."

Suddenly Smoke's voice shifted to a dry-stern command,

"Take him home!"

"Oh, Mate. Gib 'em 'nother go at it! Won't hap' gain!"

"Take him home!"

He switched to the other channel to ask,

"You see that Jude?"

"See what?"

"The bomb. They almost hit us with the friggin bomb!"

The bomb… I took a picture of the bomb! Inside-my-Spotmatic-is a picture-of-the-bomb! I am no fun on a roller-coaster. Let me off this ride!

Then I lost it. I vomited the scrumptious breakfast I shared with the Special Forces. The windows were open, so my puke flew back and plastered my face and my fatigues. Smoke need only 'smell' to know what's going on in the back seat.

"Jud' take the stick."

"Me?" I question his sanity. "You want me to fly this thing?"

"Take the stick, Jud," he repeated.

In front of me, sticking out of the floor of the plane, is a stick. I grab it and hold on 'like I'm falling off the edge of the world'!"

"Relax! Relax," I scold myself, "This plane is not as sensitive as the Huey." I made myself stop hyperventilating. Slimy vomit is everywhere.

I guide the 'Bird-Dog' up and scrape cooler air, when …my nausea is gone. Smoke's intention exactly.

He lands the plane on a small Army air strip in the shadow of the Chop Chai mountain where he and Major Hoke were assigned a room. I pulled my slimy-puke-plastered-body from the plane, when an Army Corporal assigned to detail the Bird-Dog asked,

"Next time Sir, will-you-just-bring-a-barf-bag?"

Smoke looked at the corporal and flashed his best,

"I didn't know she was going to throw up," smile.

36

The Day is Still Young

We walk to Smoke's quarters on a wooden walkway, over hard-packed dirt, when a man ran out a door screaming, "Greene... Gawd-damn it! You Air Force puke. You know better than to bring a woman in here, I'll have your balls for this!"

The irate man is screaming about me! The person of the opposite sex drenched in vomit.

Smoke ignores him and motions me to keep walking. Smoke's room is small with a very small bathroom. The shower works with a chain connected to a shower-head. One can sit on the toilet, pull a cord and shower at the same time! How convenient! The bathroom is too small for me to pull off my puke-soaked fatigues. *At least I can wash vomit out of my hair.*

My host gives me a long tee shirt and, in the stifling heat, my fatigue-top dries quickly. We thumb a ride to the O'Club at Tuy Hoa Airbase where we grab a bite to eat. The evening entertainment, a group of Filipino women wastes' no time for their 'dance-act' to gyrate the floor. Their imaginative-dance is wasted on me. I motion to Smoke, and we leave. As forward-air-controllers, Smoke and Major Hoke, are allotted a jeep that is not restricted to ten o'clock closing of Phu Hiep compound. However, it appears that Tuy Hoa AB is large enough to conceal George Hoke and the 'coveted' jeep.

Smoke turns to me with his second-best offer,

"Jud' it's after ten and the road is shut down for the night, so I can't get you back to the hospital. Hoke and I have a room here on base. It's not much, just a place to sleep."

I barley know this man, but if I read his thoughts correctly, he is probably thinking, *Not much else to do but share out sleeping quarters with her. Jeeze! I didn't take her to raise!*

I interrupt his train of thought, apologize and say,

"Sleep rules. I didn't sleep well last night. I am on the short side of the 91st work schedule, as I report to duty in less than 24 hours."

I am tired, still I feel Smoke can be trusted, like the guys of the 309th were honorable. It seems an eternity, when a 'Hun" formation blocked a clear blue sky and my friends, flew the first leg of the flight back to the 'world.' It was a memorable sight. I know the memories shared with Dustys' jocks will never be replicated. *It breaks my heart.*

"What's mine is yours," Smoke says, interrupting my thoughts to hand me his toothbrush.

He shared his toothbrush, how quaint.

The gesture is heaven sent, as I haven't brushed my teeth in almost two days. Then we head to bed when, I crash in the bed on the left and Smoke crashes in the bed on the right. Luxury, an air-conditioned room. I am asleep when my head hits the pillow.

Sometime during the night I wake to the voice of a man hollering, "Greene! You couldn't screw in a whore-house, unbelievable! This is a most delectable woman, and here you be, sound asleep in separate beds!"

37

The Ravens

Morning Jud',

When we parted at Phu Hiep, I didn't have much I could say about Laos. I arrived here and was 'Sheep-Dipped' a term that means more to farmers than lovely nurses. Here's the way it happens,

I was relieved of all military gear and trappings. Last civilian breath I took was when I graduated from the Air Force Academy. I feel naked! Now I am a civilian performing a secret mission. *(You should tear this letter into small pieces and eat it!)* My life is exhilarating only because it is terrifying, Jud, please leave all evidence and military rank off correspondence.

You go on to say, "As a new Raven, Yang Bee is assigned to fly with me. I am privileged to fly my first Raven operational sortie late July 1969 with him in my backseat. He is very experienced and has excellent eyesight. This is a memorable mission for me and maybe it's a memory for Yang Bee as well. I am told he is also very cautious, and he will keep me out of trouble.

It turned out this was not correct!

I met Yang Bee at the Bird Dog. We are in flight looking for enemy activity. We are in flight, looking for enemy activity, flying at an altitude of about 3,000 feet.

When Yang Bee yanks the back of my shoulder harness to get my attention and says, *"Laven—fly to low!"*

I look back to see him looking out the left side. Curious about what he is looking at, I reduce altitude.

Keep in mind, I expect him to be "cautious," so I am not one bit bothered about danger.

He signals me to fly lower and to turn back toward a road that runs along the side of the PDJ (Plain of Jars).

As I settle down low beside the road, Yang Bee pulls my .30 caliber carbine from behind my seat and begins to fire from his window, at something on the ground. This surprises me, as I still can't see what he is shooting at.

He asks me to turn back and make another pass by the location and, "fly to low—Laven!"

Finally, I see him firing at a tank parked under the trees pointing toward us. I fly close enough to see the machine gunner in the turret firing at us. I jenk the airplane wildly around the sky while trying to gain distance from the tank. It's a miracle we did not get hit, as I'm sure we received battle damage but, when we arrive back to base, we found not a scratch. I know I said some very unkind things to Yang Bee as we headed south to our base.

I am thinking to myself that it will be a long six months if every Raven sortie is like this one. So much for the "cautious" mission we flew together.

"As for here, I love the way I can go out on any given day, do the deeds of great pilots, even foolhardy, return, have a beer and talk it over with the guys and then sack out feeling whole."

"I will be working East of Vietnam. You have to know that the mission is covert and we 'Americans' are not where I am going, however I am sure I want to be part of this mission. And it may be the mission where I may not survive. If this war is going to turn around, it may not be on our terms. I will be working to help those who have the most to lose.

Hi Jud'… Right now, I feel so glad to be alive because thirty minutes ago 'my shit was weak' It was dark, and I am near out of fuel in bleak weather. That's what I like about this job. It feels so good to do simple things, like walk on the ground and breathe fresh air. I've almost been killed every day for a careless mishap that I will never do again. Oh well. I don't have much to say Jude. I can't say much about work and there isn't anything to say about play. I may get a fighter when I leave here, but the down-side is that we are quickly running out of war.

This 'Moratorium Bullshit' hasn't helped me say this either. You can't quit having wars just because people die in them. I want to live more than any of those peace assholes. I get up in the morning wondering if 'today is the day' and at night I feel like a million bucks because it wasn't.

Judy, yesterday another Misty-Fac went in. They never heard from them, weather was bad, and they probably hit a mountain by the tri border. Pat Carol, a friend of mine from the Academy, went-in with it and the Misty Squadron Commander was with him. The Misty Commander was Col. Whitford. Wish it could have been a lot of other people Jud'… That's all I know.

38

Letter from a Patient

Dear Judy,

Just want you to know that you were a bright light during a very dark tour of duty. Before my twentieth birthday, I had been wounded in action three times. The worst injury was the multiple GSW that brought me to your hospital. I simply want to say "thank You" for your care, concern and kind words spoken daily during that six-week period. You were truly an angel existing in a living hell

Certainly, you came in contact with many wounded soldiers and there was nothing particularly outstanding that would cause you to remember me. Perhaps this will help to jog your memory. Next to the nurses' desk was a Korean soldier. He was asleep and both his eyes were bandaged. Next to his bed was a stack of Korean C-Rats (field rations) The cookies in the Korean C-Rats drove you to almost get into them. Your only fear was, "I might lose my hand as he might just come at me with a swift Korean karate chop."

For me, you were not only the first American woman I had seen in seven months, but a great source of inspiration in an otherwise depressing environment. Thanks, does not cover my gratitude. Just know that here is one soldier that would have gone the mile for you.

Ron Smith
101st Airborne
Screaming Eagle

39

Leaving Vietnam

When our flight was told to buckle in for landing in California, the soldiers and sailors on the plane didn't even hear the request. All the windows were packed with the men getting their first look of the "World."

I heard one guy say, "I hope to God that Golden Gate Bridge is not just painted on the window. . . as I was afraid, I would not come back home alive."

At San Francisco International Airport, I was harassed by a ten-year-old boy. I didn't hold it against him, as he was talking in public what his mother said in private.

I reported for duty at Fitzimmons Army Hospital in Denver. I asked to work on the Orthopedic Ward, but instead I served on the Neurosurgical Ward. When an opening to transfer became available, I declined, as by then I had fallen in love with the patients on the Neruo Ward.

Most of my patients suffered damage to their spinal cord. These men faced an uphill battle and would deal with challenges they had never imagined. On the plus side, they had their families, they had each other, and they had the resilience of youth.

Carol and I planned an evening for a couple of paraplegic patients. Somehow, we managed to get them and their wheelchairs into my Datsun station wagon. Then we hit the road to enjoy an evening away from the hospital. Our evening included dinner at a pub in downtown Denver.

Getting our two guys out of the car and into their wheelchairs should have been a struggle. I considered it a privilege. In we rolled, with Carol pushing a guy in a wheelchair, and I doing the same right along behind her. We all four were settled at a table when a man from a table nearby came and talked to us. He learned that the two guys in wheelchairs were wounded in Vietnam, and Carol and I were Army nurses. Then he turned and went back to his table. The waitress said, "y'all should just order whatever you want, as the men at that table over there said for me to tell you to 'put your wallets away,' that 'your money is no good here.' "

As a Vietnam Veteran, I, along with thousands of others, had hidden our Vietnam service from the angry people in our nation. No protestor will ever erase the memory of the WWII Veterans, to four Vietnam Veterans, that evening at the restaurant, when they told us, "Put your wallets away, because your money is no good here."

40

Hello 'Grunt'

Tuy Hoa Air Base, Vietnam
Hi "Grunt"
July 16,1969

    I have an ulterior motive for writing this letter as you will soon see. First however let me announce that 'Dusty's Tavern" hasn't been the same since you left. Ever since we lost the steadying influence of a 'real-live-Round-Eyed-Girl' the boys are getting rowdy. There has been glass throwing and profane language etc.
    Only a few exciting things have happened since you left. Bill Lloyd managed to fly an airplane through the trees N.W. of Pleiku and in accordance with Wing policy he was immediately grounded. Both Col. Carr and I fought that without success. Col. P was very set in his ways, so Bill has had his last mission in good ole' Vietnam. Then believe it or not George "Hoke" did the same thing. He's now on 89 days TDY to 7th AF. Both are lucky to be alive. Bill landed his Hun at Pleiku and Hoke at Ben Hoa. At least

they got on the ground. I haven't seen Hoke's airplane, but Bill's is a mess! We'll get it flying again eventually but it is going to take about two months.

Then last night Butch Brady had the engine stop running for unknown reasons on a pass just south of Cambodia and he jumped out. He was picked up in about 20 minutes by an Army Huey with not even a scratch. He even flew the next day. All in all, things have been exciting.

Now to the incident that reminded me of you and the real purpose of this letter. I don't know if you remember my mentioning it or not, but my dad is or was a college baseball coach in Iowa, Cedar Falls to be exact. He had a ball player on his team who was here in Vietnam when we were here. Stationed near or at Dak To. The kid was shot up bad and is in Fitzsimmons Army Hospital in Denver. His name is John Nelson Spc 4 class or perhaps higher. He may have been promoted by now. Anyway, I thought it would do him good if you can locate him in that 'disease emporium' and say "hi" just tell him that "Mon" Whitford's son wanted you to say 'hi.' " Mon" is my dad's nickname and he's been worried about the kid. If he is gone by now or you are too busy, don't worry about it, but I thought it might do him some good to have a pretty girl walk in and say hello. Thank you, Florence Nightingale.

Well Judy girl, I think I've about covered the news from here. If you can find the time, drop us a line as we all would like to know how you are doing. Try to not break a leg on the ski slopes and have a ball Judy girl.

Yours for bigger and better wars
Larry. Lt. Col L.W.Whitford
309th TFS CMR 3725 APO SF 96316

LTC Larry Whitford died when his 'Hun' when down in Vietnam, close to Laos. I penned a letter to his wife, Jo Whitford, and sent her a picture of her husband. She lived in Texas.

Dear Judy,

Thank you for the slide, looks so familiar, a very good picture. Thank you for taking time to write a sweet letter. I appreciate it. Time is helping me, but I still have a long way to travel before I can trail a flying suit or a 'dirty ole pair of flight boots' and it doesn't bring a knot to my stomach and throat. They reached the crash site in April. They found no trace of seats or bodies or pieces of bodies. It appears that they were not in the plane at impact. Their chances of survival have gone up 75%. I have been in Richardson, Texas for a month. It is a suburb of Dallas. It has many shopping centers and a good school system. I am a Texan and enjoy the climate here. Larry and I have two children, Larry III who is 14 and Nancy who is 12. Life is so busy when you have teen-agers and it is fun. They keep you on your toes. I am grateful that you include us in your prayers. We will need all the help we can get any of our men back. Again, thank you being so thoughtful.

Sincerely,
Jo Whitford

I penned a letter to the family of one of my patients. On August 20, 1968, I received from her this thank-you:

Dear Miss Crausbay,

We want to thank you from the bottom of our hearts for your letter concerning our son, Daniel. We were sick with worrying, not knowing the facts. I pray to God that he will be alright, and God bless you for your kindness.

Sincerely,
Mrs. Connell

I prayed an ancient Irish prayer over the men and women and their families, whose lives were changed by the war in Vietnam

May the road rise to meet you
May the wind be always at your back
May the sunshine warm upon your face.
And the rains fall soft upon your fields
And until we meet again
May God hold you in the palm of his hand

41

Epilogue

You have read my book. It was about the fear, the courage and the comical scenes in the lives of those near me. I purposively didn't pen the blood and gore of the Vietnam war. Lives were changed; many lives were forever changed. As a Vietnam Veteran, I, along with thousands of others, hid our Vietnam service from the angry people in our nation.

Thirteen years have lapsed since my sister's death. When she died, I walked away from friendship with Jesus. In 1976, I am the mother to my first born, a beautiful baby girl. One day, I held her up in the mirror and I talked to the baby in the mirror, "You deserve a better mother than me!" The journey back to the Lord was not easy as had to let Vietnam go; I had to forgive LBJ and Robert McNamara. Forgiving the politicians was hard, as many young lives slipped through our hands. Needlessly. Today I celebrate the good in life; my daughter and my son live nearby. They call me Mom, and six Grands call me Nana.

Made in the USA
Monee, IL
30 June 2021